Creating and Managing a CRM for your Organisation

More than ever, organisations are facing a data avalanche from various sources, be they in electronic or hard copy format. How an organisation manages this ever-increasingly important resource – data – can benefit or hinder its ability to achieve its objectives.

Creating and Managing a CRM Platform for your Organisation not only covers how the principles of data management, including data quality and data security, can be applied to an organisation's customer relationship management (CRM) platform, but also highlights how aspects of data management, marketing and technology are needed to operate, develop and manage a CRM platform in order to carry out tasks such as reporting and analysis, developing data plans, undertaking data audits, data migrations and campaign mailings that will result in an organisation using data effectively in order to achieve its goals and objectives. The issues and topics covered apply to all organisations that use a CRM platform and the data it contains as part of their business activities, regardless of the industry sector or size of the organisation.

A comprehensive overview of the practices that can be effectively implemented when managing a CRM platform, this book is essential reading for professionals involved in the administration of the CRM platform within their organisation and data management.

Richard Boulton has undertaken CRM platform data projects and has administered CRM platforms in a variety of industry sectors, including not-for-profit, financial services and government.

Creating and Managing a CRM Platform for your Organisation

Richard Boulton

Routledge
Taylor & Francis Group

LONDON AND NEW YORK

First published 2019
by Routledge
2 Park Square, Milton Park, Abingdon, Oxon OX14 4RN

and by Routledge
52 Vanderbilt Avenue, New York, NY 10017

Routledge is an imprint of the Taylor & Francis Group, an informa business

British Library Cataloguing in Publication Data
A catalogue record for this book is available from the British Library

Library of Congress Cataloging-in-Publication Data
Names: Boulton, Richard, 1973- author.
Title: Creating and managing a CRM platform for your organisation / Richard Boulton.
Description: Abingdon, Oxon ; New York, NY : Routledge, 2019. | Includes bibliographical references and index.
Identifiers: LCCN 2018034598| ISBN 9781138335783 (hardback) | ISBN 9781138335806 (pbk.) | ISBN 9780429443534 (ebook)
Subjects: LCSH: Customer relations—Management—Data processing. | Management information systems.
Classification: LCC HF5415.5 .B68 2019 | DDC 658.8/12—dc23
LC record available at https://lccn.loc.gov/2018034598

ISBN: 978-1-138-33578-3 (hbk)
ISBN: 978-1-138-33580-6 (pbk)
ISBN: 978-0-429-44353-4 (ebk)

Typeset in Times New Roman
by Swales & Willis Ltd, Exeter, Devon, UK

Contents

Figures

Copyright acknowledgements and author credits

I would like to take this opportunity to thank the following people, without whose support and help I would have been unable to write this book.

I thank all the people at Routledge who have guided, supported and helped me publish this book and the publishers that have given me permission to use extracts from their authors' work, including the following:

Larry P. English (2009), *Information Quality Applied Best Practices for Improving Business Information, Processes, and Systems* (Wiley) – No part of this publication may be reproduced, stored in a retrieval system or transmitted in any form or by any means, electronic, mechanical, photocopying, recording, scanning or otherwise, except as permitted under Sections 107 or 108 of the 1976 United States Copyright Act, without either the prior written permission of the Publisher, or authorization through payment of the appropriate per-copy fee to the Copyright Clearance Center, 222 Rosewood Drive, Danvers, MA 01923,(978) 750–8400, fax (978) 646–8600. Requests to the Publisher for permission should be addressed to the Permissions Department, John Wiley & Sons, Inc., 111 River Street, Hoboken, NJ 07030, (201) 748-6011, fax (201) 748-6008, or online at http://www.wiley.com/go/permissions.

DataFlux Corporation (2003), *Data Profiling: The Foundation for Data Management* – Copyright © 2004, SAS Institute Inc., Cary, NC, USA. All Rights Reserved. Reproduced with permission of SAS Institute Inc., Cary, NC.

Keith Baxter (2010), *Risk Management* (Pearson Education Limited) – All rights reserved. No part of this publication may be reproduced, stored in a retrieval system, or transmitted in any form or by any means, electronic, mechanical, photocopying, recording or otherwise, without either the prior written permission of the publisher or a licence permitting restricted copying in the United Kingdom issued by the Copyright Licensing Agency Ltd, Saffron House, 6–10 Kirby Street, London EC1N 8TS. This book may not be lent, resold, hired out or otherwise disposed of by way of trade in any form of binding or cover other than that in which it is published, without the prior consent of the Publishers.

Creating and Managing a CRM Platform for your Organisation contains public sector information licensed under Open Government License 3.0 (www.nationalarchives.gov.uk/doc/open-government-licence/version/3/).

Trademark acknowledgement

1 Introduction

More than ever, organisations are facing a data avalanche from various sources, be they in electronic or hard copy format. How an organisation manages this ever-increasingly important resource which is data can benefit or hinder its ability to achieve its objectives.

This book has been written as a guide on how to implement, administer and develop a CRM database platform and use data effectively to meet organisational objectives.

It was developed to educate and inform professionals who would like to improve their knowledge of data management and to provide staff who are responsible for managing their organisation's CRM platform with ideas and practical advice to develop best practices by combining technology, data management and marketing principles.

With the implementation of best practices, a CRM platform can bring benefits to an organisation, including:

- providing an aid to meet business objectives more effectively;
- improving efficiency of the CRM database within the organisation;
- eradicating duplicated work;
- improving workflows within the organisation;
- addressing legal and compliance issues surrounding data within the organisation.

The issues and topics covered in this book will apply to all organisations that use a CRM platform and the data it contains as part of their business activities regardless of the industry sector or the size of the organisation.

This is not a technical book on how databases are designed and does not advocate the use of one database platform or another, but it is a general overview of the tasks and issues involved when managing a CRM platform.

As this book is concerned with databases, it inevitably uses some technical jargon and IT terminology. These terms will be explained as they occur in a way that non-technical users and readers will understand.

Contents of the book

The book is divided into three parts.

Part I: Overview of data and CRM platforms

This part of the book introduces the reader to the concepts and theory behind the practical measures an organisation can implement in order to manage and administer an effective CRM platform.

It includes concepts such as:

- defining data – the difference between data and information;
- the data lifecycle – the stages data goes through, including collection, maintenance, analysis and reprocessing;
- types of CRM platforms – what types of CRM platforms in the marketplace can be implemented in an organisation.

Part II: Implementing a CRM platform

This part covers:

- the factors to consider when developing a CRM platform;
- the project management process of implementing a CRM platform in an organisation.

Part III: CRM data administration data issues and tasks

This part covers issues related to the data within the CRM database, including:

- data quality;
- data capture;
- data plans;
- data security;
- organisation of the data team;
- data migrations;
- data security;
- reports and analysis;
- data legislation;
- mailings;
- data suppliers;
- data storage.

Data scenarios

The book also provides case studies of data scenarios set in a fictitious organisation, Data XYZ PLC, to highlight how an organisation can improve its data practices and better manage its data.

The Data XYZ PLC marketing department comprises four teams:

- business development section;
- digital and creative team;
- marketing team;
- sales team.

The heads of department directly report to the head of marketing and are responsible for the management of their own staff.

The CRM platform is currently situated within the business development section, has an administrator managing the system, and is line-managed by a business development officer (see Figure 1).

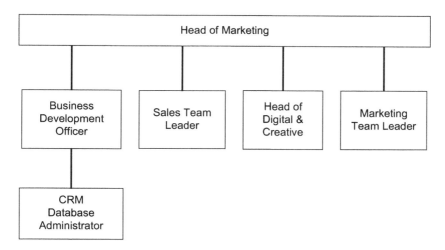

Figure 1 Marketing department of Data XYZ PLC

2 Target audience of this book

The target audience of this book includes:

- professionals responsible for administering and managing the CRM platform within an organisation;
- professionals requiring an overview of how to start to implement best data practices when managing a CRM database platform and the data it holds;
- professionals who are thinking about implementing a CRM platform within their organisation and need an overview of what factors should be considered to achieve this;
- professionals who require an overview of how data management is combined with marketing principles to achieve business objectives;
- professionals responsible for implementing data management practices within their organisation;
- professionals requiring an overview of the issues surrounding data within their organisation;
- marketing professionals who wish to gain a better understanding of how the data within the CRM platform can be managed and used more effectively.

3 Outcomes of this book

After reading this book, the reader should be able to:

- understand the importance of data and data management within a organisation;
- improve and implement data practices in administering and managing the CRM platform in order to efficiently and effectively use the data within the database;
- understand the data tasks and processes involved in the management and operation of a CRM platform in order to meet organisational goals;
- understand how data management principles can be applied to the management of a CRM platform within an organisation.

Part I
Overview of data and CRM platforms

Part I will cover:

- the data lifecycle;
- defining what data is;
- defining a CRM platform;
- the types of CRM platform that can be implemented within an organisation;
- process mapping within an organisation;
- aspects involved in data management within an organisation.

4 Overview of data and CRM platforms

This chapter will cover some basic background data knowledge the reader should be aware of before reading this book.

Defining data

The terms 'data' and 'information' seem to be interpreted by people as having the same meaning and being interchangeable.

A model used to explain the difference between data and information is outlined by DAMA (2009, pp.2–3)[1] as Data, Information, Knowledge and Wisdom (DIKW).

Data, as stated by DAMA (2009, p.2),[2] can be defined as: 'the representation of facts as text, numbers, graphics, images, sound or video'.

Information gives that data meaning in some sort of context, as outlined by DAMA (2009, p.2).[3]

In this case, organisations apply some sort of meaning to the data – for example, 109 could be a transaction number for one organisation, but to another organisation it could mean a user ID.

Knowledge involves understanding and gaining insight into this information, as outlined by DAMA (2009, p.3),[4] and will lead to wisdom.

Definition of a CRM platform

If you look through any marketing literature, I'm sure it will give you a definition of what customer relationship management is all about. What, however, does this have to do with CRM platforms?

Customer relationship management is all about understanding customers within the marketplace in order to meet and exceed their expectations, which will help achieve organisational objectives.

---

1 *DAMA-Data Management Body of Knowledge* ©.
2 *DAMA-Data Management Body of Knowledge* ©.
3 *DAMA-Data Management Body of Knowledge* ©.
4 *DAMA-Data Management Body of Knowledge* ©.

Information needs to be collected from various data sources about customers and businesses within the marketplace so that the organisation can effectively target its goods/services/communication message in order to meet its goals.

The characteristics and features of a CRM platform that may feature in any definition include the following:

- A CRM database can be defined as a system for storage, processing, maintenance and reporting/analysis of information in order to meet marketing and business objectives.
- It assists in marketing tasks like campaign management and delivery, event management, contact management, reporting and analysis, and marketing functions like business development, customer service, sales and marketing in order to meet marketing objectives.
- It is able to provide and store transactional, behavioural, personal and social information on an organisation, customer or supplier, and is able to supply that information to the right person at the right time.
- A CRM platform can be a standalone system, or integrated and combined with other technologies to provide the organisation with a picture of the business environment it operates in so that the right decisions can be made to meet the organisation's objectives.

Here are the main points to be drawn from these characteristics:

- The CRM platform will support the work that is being carried out within the organisation to meet its objectives by collecting and analysing data on its customers.
- How the CRM platform is integrated will vary from one organisation to another, and the features of the CRM platform will vary depending on the requirements of the organisation.

The data process – 'the data lifecycle'

There are four main areas in the data process, or as it as better known, 'the data lifecycle', as shown in Figure 2:

1   Data capture (collection) of data – data will be collected from a variety of sources. These can include electronic sources such as text, email, websites, live data feeds, social networking sites, third-party data suppliers and other databases, or information that is in a hard copy format.
2   Storage/processing/maintenance of data – the information collected needs to be stored, maintained and processed. This stage includes looking after the data, ensuring it is kept updated and clean, processing the data for events and mailings, ensuring that the database and the information within it are secure, and optimising database performance.

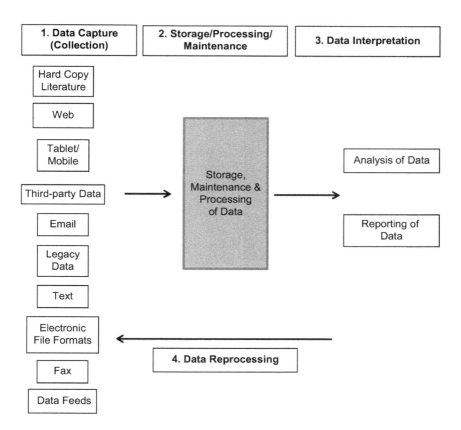

Figure 2 The data lifecycle

The data can be enriched by combining data sets or by undertaking research in order to add or find missing information amongst the records stored within the CRM platform.

This is to ensure that all information about a particular record is available to users.

Obsolete and unused data can be discarded or archived.

3   Data interpretation (analysis, interpretation and reporting) – this is where all the information in the database is analysed, interpreted and reported so that business decisions can be made by the organisation to meet business objectives.

Examples of analysis, interpretation and reporting that can be carried out on the data within the CRM platform include the reporting of performance indicators within the organisation, identifying trends and new market segments, and the analysis of campaigns executed by the organisation.

4   Reprocessing of data – after the data has been analysed and the results interpreted, the entire cycle is repeated. Data is deleted, archived, updated, requested, collected and processed.

The entire process could be viewed as a machine. It takes raw information from various sources, and the data is processed and turned into something tangible that an organisation can use to meet its objectives.

How effective this 'data machine' is depends on how efficiently it is designed and administered.

The front-line task of making sure the database is as effective as possible is the responsibility of the data team/CRM database administrator.

However, the entire organisation should be involved in ensuring the machine is as effective as possible.

With the correct technology, management and organisational attributes in place, real-time data processing, validation and reporting can be achieved to create the most efficient 'data machine' to help achieve an organisation's goals and objectives.

Other sources of data

Other data sources such as government statistics and open data sources are available, but these are not necessarily stored in a CRM platform.

The information stored in a CRM platform represents the 'touch points' where the organisation interacts with its customers and/or other businesses.

Areas of data management

Three main areas will be involved when assessing and improving data management within an organisation and data team. The framework that will be used to discuss the areas of data management is:

- technology;
- data mapping and processes;
- people.

This framework has been used in the field of information technology security, as described in 'People, Process and Technology' (Schneier, 2013).

Technology

This section will describe the technologies – the types of CRM platforms and data services – available to organisations.

Types of database platform that can implemented within an organisation

In the CRM database marketplace, there are broadly three types of CRM platforms an organisation can implement.

Open source database platforms

These are database platforms available on the Web that can be downloaded and implemented within the organisation.

Bespoke/in-house systems

These CRM platforms are completely designed and built by the organisation itself from scratch and customised to meet its needs.

Off-the-shelf packages

There are broadly two types of off-the-shelf packages that can be purchased:

a) industry-specific – some business sectors have CRM platforms specifically designed for the industry the business operates in; the not-for-profit and legal sectors have a range of platforms specifically designed for them;
b) general-purpose CRM platforms that can be customised – even though these CRM platforms are aimed at the sales and marketing environment, they can be customised to meet the needs of an organisation regardless of the industry it operates in.

Related CRM technologies and services

Cloud services

There are also cloud-based data and software solutions that can be used by an organisation.

Software as a service is when the software is hosted by a third-party provider in the cloud. The organisation accesses the software – in this case, the CRM platform hosted by the third-party provider – across a secure internet connection.

Other data services available via the cloud that could be used by an organisation in the development of a CRM platform include:

*   data as a service;
*   analytics as a service;
*   database as a service;
*   security as a service;
*   infrastructure as a service.

Data services

Data services such as data cleaning and processing financial information can be outsourced to third-party suppliers and providers. Third-party providers may even be able to provide the organisation with data lists for marketing purposes.

Data consultancy services that deal with specific data issues like quality, security, governance and legislation are also available should the organisation require these types of services.

Artificial intelligence (AI)

AI applications are being developed and integrated into CRM platforms.

Data mapping and processes

The implementation of technological solutions to resolve data problems is only one aspect of improving data management within an organisation.

Data processes need to be reviewed and mapped to improve their execution within a team and organisation.

The types of process mapping that will be covered are flowchart, cross-functional process map and relationship map, as outlined by Premier Inc. (2013).[5]

Flowcharts

A flowchart is a map that outlines the stages, steps or phases that are undertaken to complete a specific task.

Flowcharts have their own notations to illustrate where tasks, decisions and actions occur within the overall process.

The reasons for producing flowcharts, some of which are outlined in Premier Inc. (2013),[6] include:

- serving as a training aid for new members of staff;
- acting as a catalyst for agreement between teams and internal departments about how work should be carried out within an organisation;
- highlighting problem areas within a process;
- showing the differences between the ideal and actual flow of the process within an organisation;
- identifying areas where more information needs to be collected and researched;
- highlighting areas for improving processes within the organisation by simplifying and standardising tasks, and reducing repetitive loops and redundant tasks that do not need to be included in the overall process.

Flowcharts are concerned with the process of specific tasks within an organisation or team.

The main points of flowcharts are outlined by Premier Inc. (2013):[7]

- Flowcharts show the different stages the organisation needs to go through to complete a task.
- They do not show who within the organisation undertakes the different tasks within the process.
- Flowcharts do not show the relationships between the organisation and external agencies.

5 Premier Inc. (2013), *Examples of Types of Process Maps*, Charlotte, NC: Premier Inc.
6 Premier Inc. (2013), *Examples of Types of Process Maps*, Charlotte, NC: Premier Inc.
7 Premier Inc. (2013), *Examples of Types of Process Maps*, Charlotte, NC: Premier Inc.

Cross-functional charts

A cross-functional chart shows the steps within a process and who should undertake particular tasks.

The main points of cross-functional charts are outlined by Premier Inc. (2013):[8]

- They show the steps or tasks involved in the process and who performs each of them.
- They show the relationships between the organisation and external agencies and suppliers.
- They ask the following questions, as outlined by Premier Inc. (2013):[9]

  What steps are performed within a particular process?

  Who performs these steps?

Relationship maps

Relationship maps show which parts of the organisation are connected to other parts of the organisation, the different flows into and out of an organisation, and how the organisation is related to other external suppliers/agencies.

The main points of relationship maps are outlined by Premier Inc. (2013):[10]

- Relationship maps do not show the processes between the different functions.
- Relationship maps show the relationships between the different parts of the organisation.
- Relationship maps show the connections the organisation has with external agencies.
- Relationship maps set out what the organisation provides to external agencies as well as internal departments/teams/business functions.

Generating process maps

Maps of how individuals, teams and the organisation operate can be developed and produced by undertaking business analysis and using research methodologies such as questionnaires, work-shadowing staff and reviewing business documentation.

People

This area of data management is concerned with the human aspect of the data organisation: how staff are trained, motivated, managed and organised to ensure data tasks and processes are effectively carried out to achieve organisational goals.

---

8 Premier Inc. (2013), *Examples of Types of Process Maps*, Charlotte, NC: Premier Inc.
9 Premier Inc. (2013), *Examples of Types of Process Maps*, Charlotte, NC: Premier Inc.
10 Premier Inc. (2013), *Examples of Types of Process Maps*, Charlotte, NC: Premier Inc.

Summary

There are four main areas of the data process where a CRM platform can assist an organisation:

- capture (collection) of data;
- storage, processing and maintenance of data;
- analysis, interpretation and reporting of information;
- data reprocessing.

Implementing technological solutions to improve data management within an organisation and marketing department is only one aspect of data management.

Processes and the people involved in the management of the CRM platform and data within an organisation must also be assessed, developed and continually improved.

There are a wide range of database platforms available in the marketplace. However, there are broadly three main types of systems:

- open source platforms;
- bespoke in-house-developed CRM platforms;
- off-the-shelf packages.

Part II

Implementing a CRM platform

Part II will cover:

- the project management lifecycle of implementing a CRM platform in an organisation;
- the types of project management methodologies that can be used to implement and develop the CRM database on an ongoing basis;
- some of the issues and problems when implementing a CRM platform in an organisation.

5 Implementing a CRM platform

This chapter deals with the process of implementing a CRM platform within an organisation.

The process will:

- help the organisation identify the type of CRM platform it will implement;
- establish an implementation methodology for the CRM database within the organisation.

CRM implementation process

In order to implement a CRM database, a project management process needs to be developed within the organisation.

A project management process can be defined as a systematic approach or sequence that comprises of a number of steps/phases that an organisation/team will go through in order to complete a task, goal, objective or specified piece of work.

The number of steps or the process employed to complete this work are completely up to the organisation.

Some project methodologies have their own clearly defined phases and steps, but this is by no means the only way of managing a project.

Organisations have the choice of:

- following a defined project management methodology;
- implementing their own project management process.

Note: The project management process and steps used in this text do not follow a standard or recognised project management methodology.

These steps do, however, follow and have similarity to the System Development Lifecycle set out by DAMA (2009, p.4),[1] which follows the phases of:

- Plan;
- Analyse;
- Design;

1 *DAMA-Data Management Body of Knowledge* ©.

- Build;
- Test;
- Deploy;
- Maintain.

They also draw on other documents, such as *The Six Elements of Successful CRM Selection and Implementation: How to Stay Focused and Cover Your Bases When Choosing and Setting Up a Customer Relationship Management System*' by Leland and Salter, FivePaths, LLC (n.d.)[2] and Epicor (2005).[3]

The process and steps that will be used in this example to implement a new CRM system within an organisation are:

1   planning;
2   business analysis/audit;
3   business requirements;
4   assessing and choosing the solution;
5   development and production of the CRM platform;
6   evaluating and testing the CRM platform;
7   implementation and deployment of the CRM platform within the organisation;
8   ongoing support work;
9   review/feedback and closing the project.

The process is outlined in Figure 3.

Developing a business case and initiating the project

Some people reading this book may believe that the first stage of the project management lifecycle is initiating the project.

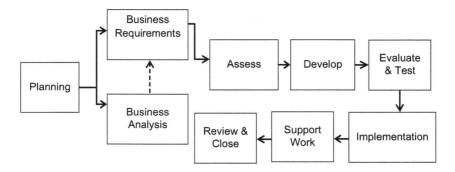

Figure 3 A project management process

2 Leland, E. and Salter, J., FivePaths, LLC (n.d.), *The Six Elements of Successful CRM Selection and Implementation: How to Stay Focused and Cover Your Bases When Choosing and Setting Up a Customer Relationship Management System*. https://www.fivepaths.com/sites/default/files/resources/six_elements_of_successful_crm_selection_and_implementation-fivepaths.pdf.
3 Epicor (2005), *Strategies for a Successful CRM Implementation: A Guide for Small and Medium Sized Enterprises*, Irvine, CA: Epicor Software Corporation.

For this text, it will be assumed that the organisation has already gone through the process of making a business case and someone has successfully made the argument for the introduction/development of a CRM platform.

Each organisation will have its own process for evaluating the need to implement new systems and technologies, but each project will be evaluated on:

- the benefits it can bring to the organisation;
- the increased effectiveness introduced into the organisation by the implementation of the new technology.

These will be outlined and documented against any associated costs for the project.

An objective evaluation can then be undertaken to decide whether the project should be approved and initiated.

1. Planning

How resources such as people and material are allocated in relation to the time available to complete the project needs to be evaluated and considered, and finally a plan implemented, if the overall objective is to be achieved.

Types of plans

The types of plans that need to be developed in order for the project to succeed and to control the main areas of the project include:

- communications plans;
- cost and financial planning;
- risk planning;
- process planning;
- schedule planning;
- resource planning;
- contingency planning.

Project management planning overview

Some of the issues that will be covered in these plans that will lead to the successful implementation of the CRM platform are worth covering in greater depth.

OBJECTIVES

The organisation will need to define the overall objectives of the project. Objectives need to be SMART (Specific, Measurable, Achievable, Realistic and Timeable).

This will form part of the evaluation of the CRM platform project and define whether it has been a success or failure.

Overall objectives may include:

- project-related objectives in terms of cost and time;
- measuring the effectiveness of the CRM platform when it has been implemented;
- objectives defined in the original business case for implementing the CRM platform.

STAKEHOLDERS AND PROJECT TEAM

The stakeholders can be internal or external to the organisation, or a combination of both, depending on the solution that is to be implemented.

The size, structure and composition of a project team will depend on the project that is to be undertaken, but will be led by a project manager who is responsible for ensuring the project is completed to agreed timelines and specifications.

CONTROLLING THE PROJECT

A project control process and system must be implemented and applied to the project.

Failure to control the project accordingly will result in:

- over-running task and schedule deadlines, which will result in the project's completion deadline being missed;
- an increase in the costs involved in the project, resulting in financial projections for the completed project not being achieved;
- inability to deliver the scope or project specification outlined at the start of the project.

Developing the types of project plans discussed earlier in this section will enable the project team to control and manage the project as it progresses.

SCHEDULES

When outlining a project schedule, the following areas need to be taken into consideration:

- how long the project will take;
- specific targets and milestones for the project to achieve and when they should be reached;
- the resources available to complete the project;
- when certain tasks and activities in the project will be started and completed.

2. Business analysis/audit

The business analysis/audit forms part of the research process that is used to select the type of CRM platform and how it will be developed within the organisation.

Business factors taken into account in a feasibility study to evaluate whether a project is feasible or not include the following.

Financial

For any project, the financial aspects and budget must be considered. This can decide whether the organisation can afford to buy an off-the-shelf CRM package or whether financial resources should be directed to developing the CRM platform internally or employing the services of a software/IT organisation to help build the CRM platform.

Different possible financial scenarios should be outlined for the CRM project in order to assist in decision-making about how the CRM platform is to be developed and implemented.

Financial considerations will cover the cost of developing the CRM platform and comparing this against the benefits of introducing the system into the organisation. Some of these financial factors and issues may have already been outlined in the business case to initiate the CRM platform project.

Comparing the costs of implementing different solutions in the organisation with the original business case can act as a decision-making tool to select an appropriate solution for the organisation.

The types of costs involved in a CRM database project that need to be considered include:

a) initial costs – what it will cost to buy/build the CRM platform;
b) ongoing costs –subscription fees, hosting fees etc.;
c) development costs – those involved in developing the system to meet organisational needs, such as hiring developers and project managers, staff and other resources.

Just because a system may be cheap to buy off-the-shelf does not mean it will be the solution that is finally chosen, as the organisation may have to spend additional funds to develop the system to customise it to meet its needs.

The different types of cost – initial, ongoing and development – need to be identified for each solution that is being considered.

A comparison of cost in conjunction with other factors should enable the business to make a decision on what platform is right for it.

Cost analysis tools such as payback can be used to make a business decision on what platform to implement based on the financial aspects of the project.

Technical

This involves looking at the technical resources of the organisation in regard to the CRM platform.

Some organisations may not have the necessary technical resources of computer programmers and developers to build, develop and maintain the CRM platform from scratch.

Technical issues may also decide whether the CRM platform is to be hosted locally or by a third-party provider.

If technical resources are unavailable to maintain the database within the organisation, a third-party-hosted solution will need to be implemented.

Marketplace

Environmental factors will affect how a business operates in the present and in the future. The business environment can be explained in terms of macro and micro environmental factors.

The macro business environment includes Political, Economic, Social, Technological, Legal and Environmental (PESTLE) factors.

The micro environment includes factors such as the marketplace, suppliers, competitors, organisation, intermediaries and customers.

These factors may help decide on what type of CRM platform is to be implemented within an organisation and how this will be carried out.

Human resources

Does the organisation have the necessary personnel to implement the CRM platform? These might be project managers, developers or programmers.

This important resource will affect the decision on the type of CRM platform implemented by the organisation.

3. Business requirements

Business requirements dictate the type of information that will be held within the database and its functionality. The business requirements of the CRM platform may be affected by the results of the business analysis.

A start can be made to gather the business requirements from the stakeholders within the organisation at the same time as the business analysis is being embarked on. Any outcomes resulting from the business analysis can then be incorporated into the final project specification of the CRM platform.

After this stage has been completed, the organisation should be able to define:

- the features and functionality the CRM platform will have after it has been developed;
- what information the CRM platform will hold;
- the technical requirements of the CRM database;
- the tasks and processes the CRM platform will be able to carry out after the system has been implemented within the organisation.

It's important that this list is compiled as this will be the benchmark for how the CRM platform is evaluated and tested, and these points will serve as criteria to judge the overall success of the implementation project.

4. Assessing and choosing the solution

After the business analysis and business requirements have been outlined, the organisation should be in a position to evaluate different CRM database solutions that will meet its business requirements.

This will mean comparing the organisation's requirements (CRM database features and functions and data requirements) with what vendors or the in-house IT team can implement.

DAMA (2009, p.141)[4] cites the decision analysis methodology of Kepner and Tregoe in *The Rational Manager* as a way of assessing the different technology options that are available to organisations.

The methodology is outlined in the following steps:

1 Understand user needs, objectives and related requirements.
2 Understand the technology in general.
3 Identify available technology alternatives.
4 Identify the features required.
5 Weigh the importance of each feature.
6 Understand each technology alternative
7 Evaluate and score each technology alternative's ability to meet requirements.
8 Calculate total scores and rank technology alternatives by score.
9 Evaluate the results, including the weighted criteria.
10 Present the case for selecting the highest-ranking alternative.

As stated earlier, the three main options/types that an organisation has to choose from are:

- develop and build the system completely internally;
- use an open source system;
- buy a complete system, and if necessary develop it to meet organisational needs.

The option selected will differ from organisation to organisation and from sector to sector, as each organisation is different and has its own unique needs and requirements.

The requirements of the organisation should be the driving force behind selecting the most appropriate CRM platform.

5. Development and production of the CRM platform

When the type of CRM platform has been chosen, the development and production process can begin.

The extent of development and production needed on the CRM platform will depend on the type of platform chosen.

Some of the aspects that need to be developed and produced broadly fall into three categories:

---

4 *DAMA-Data Management Body of Knowledge* ©.

a)   user interface – how the user interacts with the CRM application;
b)   backend systems and database design – the database holding the information needs to be designed; additional systems may need to be developed or integrated into the CRM platform, such as reporting, how emails are sent etc., depending on what the system goals and requirements are;
c)   server-/client-side scripting and development – the computer code that makes everything work needs to be developed and written.

Client-side computer code is concerned with the user interface needed to operate the CRM platform.

Server-side computer code is used to retrieve information from the database.

Another consideration could be how the CRM database interacts with other systems within the organisation. This depends on the specification of the CRM platform, and may include looking at how the CRM database interacts with reporting, financial and online marketing systems.

This is to ensure there is a single coherent process for activities like email campaigns, processing online payments and reporting on CRM database activities while ensuring the quality of the data is not compromised.

If an off-the-shelf package is to be used, it is possible that only a small amount of customisation will be necessary. This may include adding/deleting/modifying fields, changing field values or adding additional functionality to the platform.

Some CRM platforms even have their own app exchanges where this additional functionality can be downloaded for a fee or sometimes even for free.

The necessity for and scope of customisation of the CRM platform will be determined by matching and comparing the business requirements with the CRM platform the organisation has chosen.

6. Evaluating and testing the CRM platform

After the database has been built, the database and CRM platform need to be tested. The scope and extent of testing will depend on the type of CRM application implemented. There are various forms of tests that could be undertaken on the CRM platform before it is considered to be ready to be deployed in the live working environment.

Evaluating the CRM platform against the project features and business requirements list

Looking back to the start of this project management process, the organisation will have undertaken some business requirement analysis.

After the business requirement analysis had been completed, the organisation should have been able to define a list of features and tasks the completed CRM platform must be able to perform if it is to meet the organisation's needs.

The reason for this business requirement list should now be apparent.

The type of testing and the how the tests are conducted will be largely driven by the business requirements (tasks the CRM platform should be able to perform and features the platform should have to enable users to carry out their work) set out at the start of this process.

7. Implementation and deployment of the CRM platform within the organisation

When the CRM platform has been tested, it can finally be deployed in the organisation.

When implementing and rolling out the system, there are two broad approaches:

- a complete CRM implementation approach, where the system is implemented in one go;
- a phased implementation approach.

Complete CRM implementation approach

This approach requires the system to be implemented as a whole simultaneously across the organisation. For example, this approach can be used if an organisation has chosen an off-the-shelf CRM platform package.

The package will already have been designed, built and tested. The organisation may only have to undertake minor development changes such as changing field values within the database.

The system can be deployed as purchased.

Phased implementation approach

In this approach, the CRM platform is integrated into the organisation in a logical, phased manner.

A phased approach might include implementing the CRM platform according to geographic location, the features of the CRM platform, or defined business or user groups within the organisation until the entire organisation has access to the platform.

8. Ongoing support work

When the CRM platform has been implemented, some additional support work may still need to be undertaken by the project team.

Here are some ongoing tasks that may be needed to be completed before the project can be closed.

Training

There may be a need for support in training staff within the organisation, and indeed in the development of a training programme to support the implementation of the CRM platform.

Production of documentation/guidelines and processes

Any outstanding documentation will need to be written. This is to ensure that any future development work undertaken by the organisation is based on a clear understanding of what work has already been completed.

Depending on what has been outlined in the project plan, there might be a need to develop the initial processes for undertaking data tasks within the data team.

Organisational guidelines to ensure that the data team fosters a culture of best practice may also need to be developed.

Data migration

There may be a need to support the organisation in transferring data from legacy systems, various data sources and even data from the previous CRM platform used by the organisation.

Ongoing technical issues

When a system is implemented within the live environment, some unanticipated technical issues may need to be resolved.

These issues need to be dealt with before the project is brought to a close.

9. Review/feedback and closing the project

When the CRM platform has been implemented within the organisation, a period of review and feedback needs to be undertaken.

Defining when the project is closed or finished is important.

A project can be closed or declared finished when all of its objectives or the specified work outlined in the project plan have been completed.

This can be important when third parties are involved in the project.

These issues are usually outlined in any contracts between the organisation and the third-party supplier.

If third-party suppliers are involved in the CRM database, it is usual for formal project meetings and reviews to be undertaken before a project is declared closed and complete.

The closing of the project marks the end of the integration of the CRM platform into the organisation and the start of the handover phase to the organisation to manage and further develop the CRM platform to meet its needs.

The following areas need to be covered in the review and closure phase of the project.

Project performance

The success of the implementation can be evaluated in several ways. They may include:

- project metrics such as the cost and time it took to complete the project;
- the business requirements of the CRM platform;
- the overall objectives of the project.

Feedback and review

The stakeholders involved in the project will need to provide feedback on the project. This is to:

- assist in improving the project management process in the future;
- identify possible future developments that need to incorporated into the CRM system;
- improve team performance in the future;
- enable individuals working on the project to review their roles and continually develop and improve their performance and skills.

Documentation

Project documentation needs to be completed and updated so that any necessary future development work can be undertaken on the CRM platform and there is a complete and full account of the project for future reference.

Developing documentation is always ongoing, and does not stop after the CRM database has been implemented within the organisation.

Post-project development

The initial implementation of the CRM platform is the foundation stone the organisation will use to further develop the platform to meet its changing objectives and deal with its evolving business environment.

The development of the CRM platform is a continuous process. However, the same project management steps and phases used to implement the CRM platform can be employed to develop new features in order to meet any new business requirements of the organisation.

After the project has been completed and implemented, the project team and relevant stakeholders can then form part of a working group and be the focal point to continually develop the CRM platform to meet organisational needs.

User and organisational needs and the business environment the organisation operates in are always changing, therefore the CRM database must also change to meet these evolving requirements so that the organisation can meet its goals and objectives.

Project methodologies

Within project management, a number of methodologies have been developed that organisations can use to ensure that projects are managed so that project milestones, schedules and objectives are achieved.

The following methodologies could be used in the project management of implementing a CRM platform:

- Agile;
- Lean;
- Waterfall;
- Scrum;
- PRINCE2;
- Kanban.

How a chosen methodology is selected will depend upon the organisation.

Case study

Data XYZ PLC is trying to decide whether to implement a new CRM platform or whether the current CRM platform should be developed to meet the future needs of the organisation.

The organisation has a preferred supplier list.

The organisation has not defined and set out a process to enable it to make a decision on how to proceed in regard to the CRM platform.

Possible improvements to this case study scenario

It's fine that the organisation has a preferred supplier list, and this will act as good starting point for what solutions are available if the CRM platform is to be replaced.

However, the preferred supplier list is not the only solution available to the organisation, and it seems it has already decided on the possible solutions before the criteria on which the decisions are to be based have been outlined and defined.

The best solution would be the one that meets the current and future business requirements of the organisation. The business requirements for the CRM platform need to be identified. This may entail:

- liaising with various teams in the organisation, undertaking group interviews and possibly completing questionnaires to determine the system requirements of the CRM platform;
- identifying possible future needs the CRM platform will have to meet;
- clarifying the organisation's future plans and objectives in the short, medium and long term.

By the end of this stage in the process, the organisation should be able to list what the CRM system features and capabilities should include to meet its business needs.

Research could then be undertaken to find possible solutions that meet the business requirements of the organisation.

A decision should be made about how to develop the CRM platform based on the business requirements and cost analysis, looking at:

- initial costs;
- development costs;
- running costs.

In this case, the current CRM platform will be kept, but the system will be developed to meet the future needs of the organisation.

A CRM project sponsor on the board of the organisation should authorise the setting up of a project team to implement the work to upgrade the current CRM platform.

A formal project management process should be used by the organisation to implement the solution.

The project team, led by a project manager, should consist of development staff and stakeholders who have an interest in the CRM platform project.

The goals of the project should be communicated to all staff, and the benefits the work will bring should be explained.

Regular updates about how the work is progressing should be issued via the company intranet.

Any disruption the project will cause to employees should be notified by email

The new features should be trialled in a test environment before being implemented in the live CRM database environment.

Training and new documentation for the new features of the system should be developed and made available to the users of the CRM platform.

The benefits of the CRM platform should be communicated and promoted within the organisation to ensure that it is used by staff members.

To ensure that data projects and issues surrounding the CRM platform are championed within the organisation, the CRM project sponsor should be the CRM/data champion advocating and promoting the issues surrounding data and the CRM platform at board level.

If necessary, support should be provided to users within the organisation to ensure that the CRM platform and the data assets it holds are fully realised in order to achieve and even exceed the organisation's objectives.

Super-users of the CRM platform could be embedded into teams within the organisation to support staff with any problems they may be having.

When the work is completed, the working group supporting the CRM platform should deal with any issues or problems that are outstanding from the project.

Resolving these issues would act as a catalyst to drive the CRM platform forward to meet organisational needs and objectives.

Summary

This chapter has looked at the project management aspects of implementing a new CRM platform within an organisation.

The chapter has highlighted the need for a project management process to be defined for the successful implementation of the CRM platform.

The project management process and the different steps and phases that may be involved in the project management process can be summarised as follows:

- it can be defined by the organisation itself;
- a recognised project management methodology is used by the organisation to implement the CRM platform.

Once the CRM platform has been implemented, the team needs to continually develop the system so that it meets the ever-changing business requirements of the organisation.

The project management process used to implement the CRM platform within the organisation can be used to develop and introduce new features and requirements in order to meet these changing needs.

Some of the project methodologies that can be used within an organisation are:

- Agile;
- Lean;
- Waterfall;
- Scrum;
- PRINCE2;
- Kanban.

The main points for the entire process can be summed up in a simple acronym, REDCROP:

Review and feedback

Effectiveness

Decision

Customisation

Requirements

Objectives

Planning.

Review and feedback

A process of review and feedback from stakeholders in the CRM project will need to be undertaken to help assess how well the CRM project achieved its objectives.

Methods for collecting feedback on the CRM project may include:

- surveys and questionnaires;
- focus groups/CRM working groups;
- user and usability studies.

This should highlight any problems with the CRM platform that may need to be addressed and form the basis for improving it in the future.

Effectiveness

How do we measure whether the CRM platform has been a success? The criteria may include:

- sales figures;
- cost reductions;
- time effectiveness;
- improved quality of data.

The ultimate measure of how successful the CRM application has been will be whether the objectives have been achieved.

A comparison of the benefits of implementing the CRM platform with the original business case for starting the CRM project can also be carried out.

Decision

The decision to select and implement a CRM solution should be objectively based on the requirements outlined by the organisation.

The ability of the CRM platform to meet business requirements should be the driving force for implementing the chosen solution in the organisation.

Customisation

CRM applications can be customised to meet the organisation's needs and objectives.

Field values can be modified, additional fields added or different workflows implemented.

The extent of customisation of the CRM platform may depend upon factors like the chosen solution or type of CRM platform to be implemented and the platform's design specification and requirements.

No two CRM database platforms are exactly the same. The best CRM platform is the one that meets your organisation's needs and objectives.

Requirements

All CRM platforms have their own unique characteristics.

Selecting, developing and implementing the wrong CRM platform can be a costly mistake, not only in financial terms, but may also badly affect the organisation's ability to meet is goals and objectives.

It can also become a source of frustration and become detrimental to morale if employees are unable to carry out their daily tasks.

The requirements of the CRM platform must meet the present and future needs of the organisation and be able to adapt to the present and future business environment the organisation is operating in.

The requirements of the proposed solution will be derived from the analysis and research the organisation has undertaken before the decision is made on the system to be implemented.

Objectives

Objectives and system goals need to be clearly defined. Good objectives are SMART, so that they can easily be measured.

The methods used by an organisation to obtain feedback and measure effectiveness will largely depend on the objectives it has defined.

Planning

Planning needs to be undertaken not only on how to control the project, but also on what process is to be used to select, develop and implement the CRM platform.

Part III

CRM data administration issues and tasks

6   CRM data administration issues and tasks

Part III looks at core administration tasks and processes that need to be managed within an organisation for a CRM database to successfully aid the business to meet its objectives regardless of the type of CRM platform deployed.

It will cover the problems associated with these tasks and supply possible ideas and solutions in order to for the CRM database to be managed more effectively and efficiently.

The core database tasks and issues that will be addressed are:

- organisation and structure of the data team;
- data capture and data quality;
- data in relation to mailings and reports;
- data migrations;
- data plans;
- data audits;
- mailings;
- reporting and analysis;
- security;
- data storage;
- data suppliers;
- data legislation.

DATA PLANS

This section will cover:

- a framework in order to produce a data plan;
- a framework to undertake an audit on the data within the CRM platform.

The data plan process

The process of producing a data plan is based on the stages that are gone through when producing marketing plans, as outlined by Beamish (2001, p.68).[1]

The stages in the data plan process are as follows:

1 marketing audit – including a data audit;
2 SWOT analysis;
3 setting objectives;
4 determining the strategy to use;
5 implementation;
6 monitoring feedback and control.

1. Marketing audit – including a data audit

Marketing audit

A marketing audit is undertaken to look at the macro economic and micro environment an organisation operates in.

The marketing environment can be explained in terms of macro and micro environmental factors. The macro business environment includes Political, Economic, Social, Technological, Legal and Environmental (PESTLE) factors.

The micro environment includes factors such as the marketplace, suppliers, competitors, organisations, intermediaries and customers.

The marketing environment could be interpreted as becoming the organisation's data environment.

Data audit

As part of the overall audit, a data audit is undertaken to assess the organisation's or CRM platform's data assets and processes.

The framework for how to undertake a data audit outlined by Jones, Ross and Ruusalepp (2009)[2] will be used in this book to illustrate how a data audit can be conducted by an organisation.

Objectives of auditing

The objectives of an auditing process are:

* ensuring data quality standards are being achieved – this is an important attribute in what defines data quality;
* identifying any problems with the data and business rules in the CRM platform – examples could include that email addresses are not being supplied on contact records or incorrect field values are being entered into the database;

1 Beamish, K. (2001), *Marketing Operations*, Oxford: Butterworth-Heinemann, p.68.
2 Jones, S., Ross, S. and Ruusalepp, R. (May 2009), *Data Audit Framework Methodology, Version 1.8*, Glasgow, UK: HATII.

- instilling a degree of responsibility among staff using the database – actions do have consequences, and people do need to be accountable and responsible for the data within the organisation; promoting this ethos of responsibility for data in the database will help improve data quality as a whole;
- improving processes and procedures in collecting, managing and processing the data held by the organisation;
- highlighting any data gaps that need to be resolved in order for the data plan objectives to be achieved so that the overall organisational goals can be attained.

The framework of Jones, Ross and Ruusalepp (2009, pp.8–9)[3] also suggests that data audits will:

a) create efficiency savings – this will be achieved through improving systems in data processing procedures; this will give a better understanding of the organisation's future needs, such as technological infrastructure and additional data sets; the organisation will therefore be better able to plan for future needs and to budget for them;
b) enable risk management – highlighting any threats and vulnerabilities to the data held by the organisation; the appropriate action can then be taken so that the risk can be mitigated and reduced;
c) clarify access and use – finding out where data is stored could lead to improvements in how data is stored and accessed within the organisation; it could identify data assets that are being under-used or never knew existed.

As outlined by Jones, Ross and Ruusalepp (2009, p.9),[4] the aim is to ensure that the data asset value is being fully exploited.

Data audit factors

The factors of data that would be looked at in any data audit, some of which are stated by Jones, Ross and Ruusalepp (2009, p.10),[5] include:

a) data sources – where the data is being collected and obtained from;
b) data types – types of data being stored in the database;
c) type of information being collected – what actual information is being collected, such as behavioural, transactional, qualitative or quantitative information;
d) data quality – whether the information is meeting the organisation's needs;
e) data storage – how much data the organisation holds, future storage needs, and whether these can be met without compromising the performance of the database;

3 Jones, S., Ross, S. and Ruusalepp, R. (May 2009), *Data Audit Framework Methodology, Version 1.8*, Glasgow, UK: HATII.
4 Jones, S., Ross, S. and Ruusalepp, R. (May 2009), *Data Audit Framework Methodology, Version 1.8*, Glasgow, UK: HATII.
5 Jones, S., Ross, S. and Ruusalepp, R. (May 2009), *Data Audit Framework Methodology, Version 1.8*, Glasgow, UK: HATII.

f)   data usage – what data is being accessed, the frequency/time of use etc.;

g)   data processes – the effectiveness of procedures to manage and process data within the organisation.

The framework addresses five key questions, as stated by Jones, Ross and Ruusalepp (2009, p.10):[6]

1   What data assets currently exist?
2   Where are these assets located?
3   How have these been managed to date?
4   Which of these assets need to be maintained in the long term?
5   Do current data management practices place these assets at risk?

The data audit process

The framework set out by Jones, Ross and Ruusalepp (2009, p.11)[7] that is used in the data audit process has four stages:

1   planning the data audit;
2   identifying and classifying data assets;
3   assessing the management of data assets;
4   reporting findings and recommending change.

1. PLANNING THE DATA AUDIT

The planning and preparation stage of undertaking a data audit within an organisation includes as suggested by the framework of Jones, Ross and Ruusalepp (2009, pp.15–18):[8]

Timescales – how long the audit will take, and when the findings will be available for review.

Who and what will be needed to undertake the data audit – this will involve setting up the data audit team and appointing a leader who will have overall responsibility for carrying out the data audit; any resources needed by the data audit team need to be ascertained and made available.

Preparing the groundwork for the data audit – this could include notifying relevant departments or staff that a data audit will be carried out and that they may be needed to assist with it.

6 Jones, S., Ross, S. and Ruusalepp, R. (May 2009), *Data Audit Framework Methodology, Version 1.8*, Glasgow, UK: HATII.
7 Jones, S., Ross, S. and Ruusalepp, R. (May 2009), *Data Audit Framework Methodology, Version 1.8*, Glasgow, UK: HATII.
8 Jones, S., Ross, S. and Ruusalepp, R. (May 2009), *Data Audit Framework Methodology, Version 1.8*, Glasgow, UK: HATII.

The framework of Jones, Ross and Ruusalepp (2009, p.19)[9] also suggests carrying out initial background research before the start of the data audit.

Methods of auditing　The types of assets to be audited are outlined in Stage 2 of the framework of Jones, Ross and Ruusalepp (2009, pp.22–30).[10] The methods used to audit the data assets are listed below, some of which are outlined in the framework:

a) Check the data against the original set – data auditing can be as simple as checking the information against the original data set.
b) Record auditing – at a basic level, some CRM platforms have the ability to record any changes to a record in the database. This can occur manually, or the database platform can automatically log the changes to the record. This method of auditing is useful, as you are able to:

   - check that data is being entered correctly and who made the changes, and address any problems if necessary;
   - provide an audit trail if there are queries about mailing preferences from outside organisations and contacts, showing when the changes were made and who made them ;
   - rectify any errors with data imports if necessary.

c) Using SQL (Structured Query Language) queries or computer code – these can be designed and written to check the data in the database and retrieve information and statistics about the data that is held within the database. Reports can be generated to investigate the data or groups of data sets that exist/don't exist in the database and see whether measurable data quality standards within the database are being achieved.
d) Liaising with other departments and teams – this can ascertain the following information:

   - future data requirements;
   - a review of any relevant documentation;
   - data segments within the data set;
   - existing data needs;
   - future storage capacity needed to hold all the information;
   - workflows, processes and systems between departments;
   - efficiency of data processing systems within the organisation.

e) IT inventory list – the IT department may be able to provide an overview of what data is stored within the organisation. This may also include data that is held on any legacy systems and data that has been archived offsite.

---

9 Jones, S., Ross, S. and Ruusalepp, R. (May 2009), *Data Audit Framework Methodology, Version 1.8*, Glasgow, UK: HATII.
10 Jones, S., Ross, S. and Ruusalepp, R. (May 2009), *Data Audit Framework Methodology, Version 1.8*, Glasgow, UK: HATII.

f) Database schemas – these can be used to draw up a list of the type of data held within a database.

g) Database statistics – the CRM platform may be able to generate basic data statistics like the number of contacts, events, and accounts the CRM platform contains. If the CRM platform was internally developed, the IT department may be able to produce similar statistics for the types of information held in the CRM database.

h) Reviewing data processing systems and procedures – data processing systems should have been documented and can be evaluated.

i) Reviewing issue and feedback logs – records should be kept by the data team of any issues and problems encountered when undertaking data tasks. These could be technical issues when using the database or the software needed to undertake data tasks, or they could be problems encountered when undertaking data tasks and procedures if systems and workflows were found to be failing, which could indicate possible room for improvement in how work is undertaken in the future.

j) Staff interviews and questionnaires – the framework suggests conducting staff interviews and using questionnaires to identify what data assets they use and how they use them. It may also uncover data silos within individual departments and data sets the organisation never knew it had. Using these methods would also provide the opportunity for staff to discuss and review how data systems and processes are working and highlight and problems people are having in using the data to do their job, which could lead to improving the efficiency of data processes within the organisation.

k) Database monitoring tools – these can be used to analyse data usage to improve performance of the CRM platform.

l) Third-party providers – feedback from third-party data providers can be sought if the organisation uses them in processing and managing company data.

Scoping of the data audit   The scope and what will be included in the data audit needs to be defined.

The framework could be used at many levels within the organisation.

A data audit can be carried out on the entire organisation or at a departmental level.

The data audit could be carried out on all aspects of data management, including areas such as:

- data capture;
- data quality;
- data security;
- data governance.

In relation to the CRM database, the scope of the data audit initially could include:

- information held in the CRM database;
- the processes and workflows used to process and manage this information;
- assessing the quality of the data that is held in the CRM database;
- aspects of data management with regard to the CRM platform.

Later, the audit could be widened to include data held by the teams/staff that use the CRM database, which then could be widened even further to data held by departments.

As you can see from this example, an audit of one system can quickly become more complex if the scope of the data audit is not defined.

2. IDENTIFYING AND CLASSIFYING DATA ASSETS

This stage is concerned with the identification of all the data assets that fall within the scope of the data audit.

The type of assets that could be documented, as outlined by the framework of Jones, Ross and Ruusalepp (2009, pp.22–30),[11] are:

- IT inventory systems;
- databases;
- archived data sets;
- paper-based records;
- collaborative projects.

The importance of these data sets to the organisation can then be ascertained to allow further research and analysis.

The scope of the data audit will determine what assets are to be documented. An example would be the data assets relating to the CRM platform.

3. ASSESSING THE MANAGEMENT OF DATA ASSETS

This stage of the data audit involves collecting further information on the management of data sets held by the organisation.

The ultimate outcome, as stated by Jones, Ross and Ruusalepp (2009, p.31),[12] is that this 'would allow us to assess whether the current level of resources provided for management, control and curation is sufficient to maintain the value of the data asset'.

---

11 Jones, S., Ross, S. and Ruusalepp, R. (May 2009), *Data Audit Framework Methodology, Version 1.8*, Glasgow, UK: HATII.
12 Jones, S., Ross, S. and Ruusalepp, R. (May 2009), *Data Audit Framework Methodology, Version 1.8*, Glasgow, UK: HATII.

The information that could be collected about the data asset, as outlined by Jones, Ross and Ruusalepp (2009, pp.33–36),[13] includes:

- frequency of updating the data;
- owner of the data;
- purpose;
- created date;
- description of the asset;
- title;
- history of maintenance;
- file format;
- source of the data;
- users;
- back up policies;
- retention periods;
- disaster recovery policies.

Auditing systems and workflows   As part of the data audit, processes and workflows in relation to the CRM database can be audited and analysed.

The questions that arise when assessing processes and workflows may include:

- Are the processes automated or done by hand?
- Can stages in a process be combined to reduce the time it takes to complete a task?

4. REPORTING FINDINGS AND RECOMMENDING CHANGE

This stage is concerned with reporting the findings of the data audit.

The findings should be able to:

- outline any improvements the organisation can make in the data lifecycle;
- assist in identifying and filling any data gaps to help the organisation achieve its goals and objectives;
- help improve systems and workflows within the organisation;
- provide the organisation with a complete inventory of its data assets.

2. SWOT analysis

Although this is not suggested by the framework of Jones, Ross and Ruusalepp (2009),[14] the data audit could include a SWOT (Strengths, Weaknesses, Opportunities, Threats) analysis.

A SWOT analysis could be undertaken on:

---

13 Jones, S., Ross, S. and Ruusalepp, R. (May 2009), *Data Audit Framework Methodology, Version 1.8*, Glasgow, UK: HATII.
14 Jones, S., Ross, S. and Ruusalepp, R. (May 2009), *Data Audit Framework Methodology, Version 1.8*, Glasgow, UK: HATII.

- types of data the organisation holds – for example, transactional or behavioural;
- procedures and systems to manage and process data;
- the type of information the database holds – for example, qualitative or quantitative.

This combined with a SWOT analysis of the macro/internal environment would highlight any problems the organisation is experiencing in achieving its objectives

3. Setting objectives

This stage outlines the objectives the data plan needs to achieve in order for organisation to achieve its overall goals.

The objectives set should follow the SMART methodology:

- Specific
- Measurable
- Achievable
- Realistic
- Timeable.

4. Determining the strategy to use

Defining data strategy

A data strategy can be defined as the alignment of data processes, requirements, technologies and resources so that the organisation can achieve its present and future objectives in a constantly changing and evolving business environment.

DAMA (2009, p.45)[15] defines data strategy as 'a set of choices and decisions that together chart a high level course of action to achieve high level goals'.

DAMA (2009, p.46)[16] outlines the possible components of a data strategy, which may include:

- a compelling vision for data management;
- a summary business case for data management with selected examples;
- guiding principles, values and management perspectives;
- the mission and long-term directional goals of data management;
- management measures of data management success;
- short-term (12–24 months) SMART data management programme objectives;
- descriptions of data management and organisational roles along with their responsibilities and decision rights;
- descriptions of data management programme components and initiatives;
- an outline data management implementation road map (projects and data initiatives);
- scope boundaries and decisions to postpone investments and table certain issues.

15 *DAMA-Data Management Body of Knowledge* ©.
16 *DAMA-Data Management Body of Knowledge* ©.

DAMA (2009, p.46)[17] also states that a data strategy 'may also include business plans to use information to competitive advantage and support enterprise goals'.

When a strategy has been decided upon that will achieve the objectives of the data plan, the tactics the organisation will employ to ensure that the strategy will succeed can be chosen. This will ultimately help an organisation achieve its goals and objectives.

The tactics that will be used within a data strategy will cover three main areas:

- processes;
- technology;
- people.

These tactics could be applied to all areas of data management. The data management areas that would be of interest with regard to the CRM platform include:

- data capture;
- data security;
- data quality;
- data governance;
- reporting and analytics.

A gap analysis methodology could be used to highlight the differences between current data management practices identified by the initial audit and the optimal level of data management practices the organisation needs to aim for if it is to achieve its goals and objectives.

Examples of these deficiencies in current data management practices within the organisation may include the following:

- The organisation does not have specific data segments to target.
- The organisation lacks the capability to understand the results of campaigns or gain insight into the customer data it holds.
- Problems with the quality of data the organisation holds could be highlighted.

This can be best illustrated with a working example.

The organisation has decided that to achieve its goals, one of the objectives of the data plan is that it needs to implement a data quality programme with regard to the CRM platform that will improve its data in terms of defined, specified metrics and within a specific timeframe.

The organisation then adopts a strategy to achieve this objective.

After evaluating its current data quality programmes, it is found that it needs to:

- improve its CRM database training;
- introduce technological solutions to address data quality problems and issues;
- improve processes between different teams within the organisation;
- improve data capture processes.

17 *DAMA-Data Management Body of Knowledge ©.*

This outlines the development of a specific programme of work that needs to be implemented within the organisation so that it objectives can be achieved.

5. Implementation

The necessary resources –technological, financial and personnel – need to be ascertained and organised within the organisation to implement the data plan so that the objectives are achieved.

6. Monitoring feedback and control

When the tactics that are to be used by an organisation to achieve the data strategy's objectives have been implemented, the organisation's actions need to be monitored and reviewed.

After the review of the data strategy, knowledge gained from the process is fed back into the organisation, to enable it to:

- assess whether performance targets and objectives are being achieved;
- highlight areas for development and improvement within the organisation's data processes
- highlight whether the current data plan is helping to achieve business objectives.

Beamish (2001, p.77)[18] set out four key activities in controlling and monitoring plans, which will now be looked at within a data rather than a marketing context.

Development or adjustment of data (marketing) objectives

Data plan objectives will be directly determined by what the organisation has outlined as its goals and objectives.

If the objectives and goals of the organisation change, this needs to be reflected within the data plan.

Setting performance standards

Each data initiative that is implemented within the organisation will need to have some sort of performance criteria set so that it can be determined whether it is assisting in achieving the data strategy objectives.

Examples of performance standards for tasks and processes include:

- performance criteria for staff;
- technology performance standards;
- data metrics and standards.

18 Beamish, K. (2001), *Marketing Operations*, Oxford: Butterworth-Heinemann, p.77.

Evaluation of performance

Once the performance criteria for each data initiative have been determined, they need to be monitored continuously.

How performance is to be measured and evaluated can largely depend at what the organisation is trying to evaluate.

Types of evaluation that an organisation could use include:

- data profiling software;
- monitoring the data team's service level agreements;
- testing the technology that is being used within the organisation;
- financial targets and goals.

By evaluating the performance of it data initiatives, the organisation will be able to ascertain whether its data strategy is working to meet the objectives outlined in the data plan and ultimately helping to meet overall business needs.

Corrective action

When the data initiatives have been evaluated, corrective action may be needed to ensure that the objectives of the data plan are being achieved.

Corrective actions that could be undertaken depending on the results of the data evaluation could include:

- implementing new or different technology within the organisation;
- changing the workflows and processes within the organisation;
- changing the objectives of the plans for the individual areas of data management within the organisation so that they are aligned with overall organisational goals.

Data plan overview

The data plan covers the following areas:

1 What does the organisation hope to achieve in terms of goals and objectives for the data plan?
2 How does the organisation hope to achieve it?
3 What programme of initiatives will it undertake to achieve its goals?

The data plan framework outlined is a generic model that can be applied to:

- areas of data management such as data quality, data governance, and data capture etc.
- producing a data plan for the CRM platform.
- produce a data plan for the entire organisation.

These individual plans will be linked to the overall business goals. These data plans will be amended when the organisational goals and objectives are changed in relation to the organisation's evolving business environment.

Case study

Data XYZ PLC has never undertaken a data audit or outlined how it hopes to achieve its organisational objectives in the form of producing a data plan for its CRM platform.

Possible improvements in this case study scenario

The organisation needs to implement a process that will help it achieve its organisational goals by better understanding its current and future data requirements.

The organisation will implement a process to produce a data plan for the CRM platform in order to help achieve its goals. The data plan will include:

- undertaking an audit and analysis of the organisation's business environment and developing a data audit framework to assess the data held by the organisation on its CRM platform;
- outlining objectives the data plan needs to achieve so that business goals can be attained;
- how the objectives of the data plan can be achieved and implemented;
- how the data plan is to be monitored, controlled and assessed.

As part of the overall data plan process, the organisation will have to undertake and implement a data audit framework to identify and assess the data assets held on the CRM platform which will enable the organisation to compare its current data level practices to the level the organisation needs to be at to achieve its current and future objectives.

The scope of the data audit will be confined to the data in the CRM platform. However, this could act as a catalyst for a wider departmental and organisational data audits to be undertaken in the future.

The organisation could start by reviewing the system statistics – for example, how many contacts, reports, events, mailings, even segmented groups the CRM database contains – before more in-depth analysis is undertaken.

The database will be audited by assessing:

- the quality of the data;
- how relevant the data is to business needs;
- any possible data anomalies, by using data profiling tools;
- whether there are any gaps in the data sets;
- how data is segmented within the database.

As part of the audit, interviews will be conducted with members of staff which will include how they use the CRM data and database and cover all aspects of data management.

After the data has been assessed, the organisation should be in a position to:

- develop the objectives for the data plan in relation to the CRM platform;
- implement a suitable strategy to achieve these objectives.

- outline a programme of work that will help achieve the objectives of the data plan. This programme may include:

  o deleting, archiving or enriching the data within the CRM platform;
  o identifying future data requirements for the organisation;
  o identifying new ways of segmenting the database to target customers more efficiently;
  o setting up working processes with other departments to make sure data gaps do not occur and that the data meets the needs of organisation and is able to achieve its objectives;
  o identifying any developments required in the CRM platform, including the ability to hold and store the data necessary for the organisation to meet its objectives in the future;
  o identifying improvements in data processing and data workflows within the organisation;
  o producing a plan of work in all areas of data management to meet the organisation's objectives and goals.

The data audit process is carried out on a continuous basis to ensure that a culture of data improvement is adopted and high standards of data practices are maintained within the organisation.

After the data plan has been developed, the organisation needs to review its outcome and assess whether the strategy did indeed meets is overall objectives.

Issues and lessons learned from the data plan process need to be recorded and reviewed.

After reviewing the data plan, process improvements can be made to an organisation's data programmes to help achieve future goals and objectives.

Summary

It is important to implement a data plan process so that the organisation can:

- improve its data processes and workflows in relation to the CRM platform;
- objectively assess its data requirements to meet its objectives;
- instil a culture of continuous improvement of its data and data processes.

The steps that need to be undertaken in order to produce a data plan can be based on the stages that are gone through in order to produce marketing plans.

Data plans can be written for all aspects of data management, such as:

- data quality;
- data capture;
- data security;
- data governance.

The data plan needs to be driven by the overall objectives of the organisation.

When the objectives of the organisation change, the data plan should be modified accordingly to meet these new goals.

By the end of the data plan process, the organisation should be able to answer the following questions:

1   What does the organisation hope to achieve in terms of goals and objectives for the data plan?
2   How does the organisation hope to achieve its goals and objectives as outlined in the data plan?
3   What tasks is the organisation going to undertake to achieve its goals and objectives?
4   How will the data plan be reviewed and monitored.

An important stage of the data plan process is undertaking an audit of the organisation's data.

The data audit framework of Jones, Ross and Ruusalepp (2009, p.11)[19] includes the following stages:

1   planning the audit;
2   identifying and classifying data assets;
3   assessing the management of data assets;
4   reporting findings and recommending changes.

Data auditing and the production of reports on the quality of data and data practices should be undertaken on a regular basis to identify potential problems and issues with the data in the database, including the identification of data gaps, so that solutions can be implemented and the quality and integrity of the data is maintained to a high standard.

Data audits need to include an audit of not only the data assets and sets the organisation holds, but also the processes, workflows, procedures, guidelines and documentation the organisation uses to manage these assets.

DATA CAPTURE (COLLECTION) AND DATA QUALITY

This section will cover:

- the capture (collection) of data within an organisation;
- defining what data quality is in regard to data within the CRM platform;
- an outline of a data quality framework that can be implemented within an organisation in regard to the CRM platform;
- suggestions for improvements that can be implemented within the organisation to improve data quality within the CRM platform.

19 Jones, S., Ross, S. and Ruusalepp, R. (May 2009), *Data Audit Framework Methodology, Version 1.8*, Glasgow, UK: HATII.

We live in a data/database society where information is a commodity and where the quality of data and information held by an organisation can either be an asset or a hindrance to achieving its goals.

This section of the book looks at the issues of data capture and data quality. It will underline the importance of having high-quality data and make suggestions on how data can be improved within the CRM platform, supporting the statement that:

A CRM database is only as valuable as the information and data it holds.

Data capture (collection)

Data that is stored in the CRM database can be collected from various sources, both electronic and in hard copy format. Some of the data capture points have already been outlined in the data lifecycle.

The information collected from the various data sources has to be stored in the database, which is why the organisation has to go through the process of identifying different data types when designing the CRM platform so that the data can be collected and stored appropriately.

A data capture and collection strategy and plan need to be developed within the organisation.

The factors that need to be considered in the data capture and collection plan will include the following questions:

- How will the data be collected?
- What data will be collected?
- Where is this data going to come from?
- What technology will be used to store the information –for example, a CRM platform?

The data capture and collection process is important as:

- It is a vital part of the data quality process.
- It assists in filling data gaps – for example, discrepancies between the data in the database and the ability to achieve organisational objectives.
- It ensures that the organisation is constantly updated with relevant data and information to meet its objectives.

Data quality

This section is concerned with making sure that information collected from the various data sources is correctly recorded on the CRM platform. This ensures that the data assimilated into the database is of a high quality so that the organisation can use this valuable resource to meet its objectives.

What does data quality mean?

Before we can discuss what practical measures an organisation can undertake to ensure that its data is of a high quality, we must first define what exactly we mean by data quality.

It is not easy to define data quality, but a possible definition could be data that is appropriate and acceptable for a particular purpose or use that enables an organisation or individual to achieve stated goals and objectives. However, defining the aspects of data quality is rather difficult, and we can only say that it has many multi-dimensional aspects.

English (2009, pp.181–186)[20] sets out aspects of data quality under the following headings.

Quality characteristics of information content

These include dimensions such as:

- definition conformance;
- existence;
- completeness;
- validity;
- accuracy;
- precision;
- non-duplication;
- source quality and security warranties or certifications;
- equivalence of redundant or distributed data;
- concurrency of redundant or distributed data;
- currency.

Quality characteristics of information presentation

These include dimensions such as:

- availability;
- accessibility timeliness;
- presentation media appropriateness;
- relevance;
- presentation standardisation;
- presentation clarity;
- presentation objectivity;
- presentation utility.

DAMA (2009, pp.296–297)[21] includes the following aspects in its definition of data quality:

- accuracy;
- completeness;
- consistency;

---

20 English, L.P. (2009), *Information Quality Applied: Best Practices for Improving Business Information, Processes, and Systems*, Chichester, UK: Wiley.
21 *DAMA-Data Management Body of Knowledge* ©.

- currency;
- precision;
- privacy;
- reasonableness;
- referential integrity;
- timeliness;
- uniqueness;
- validity.

Some of these dimensions will be discussed below, along with an outline of what measures could be implemented within an organisation to improve data quality.

Timeliness

Timeliness, according to DAMA (2009, p.297),[22] 'refers to the time expectation for accessibility and availability of information'.

When discussing data quality, there is a timeframe element to its definition. Examples of when data needs to be made available within an organisation include:

- the processing of reports;
- ensuring that mailing data is retrieved and compiled in time to ensure campaign schedules are met.

The concept of the 'data lag time' needs to be considered – the time it takes to modify old information in the database to a new updated state so that it is available for use.

An example of this 'data lag time' is when data is processed manually or being imported into the CRM platform. While being processed, the data is not available to be used by stakeholders within the organisation.

Accuracy

Accuracy, as stated by English (2009, p.181),[23] can be defined as: 'The data value correctly represents the characteristic of the real world object or event it describes.'

Examples in a CRM database would be that contact details are correct for organisations and contacts, and even that the statuses of attendees at an event have been correctly marked up so the number of people attending can be ascertained.

Completeness

Completeness, as stated by English (2009, p.181),[24] can be defined as: 'Each process or decision has all the information it requires.'

---

22 *DAMA-Data Management Body of Knowledge* ©.
23 English, L.P. (2009), *Information Quality Applied: Best Practices for Improving Business Information, Processes, and Systems*, Chichester, UK: Wiley.
24 English, L.P. (2009), *Information Quality Applied: Best Practices for Improving Business Information, Processes, and Systems*, Chichester, UK: Wiley.

An example could be that a contact record needs to include a valid postal address, email and contact name.

Relevance

Relevance, as stated by English (2009, p.183),[25] can be defined as: 'The characteristic in which the information is the right kind of information that adds value to the task at hand, such as to perform a process or make a decision'.

The data collected and stored in the database needs to be relevant to the organisation's current and future objectives and needs.

If organisational objectives change, the data on the database may need to change to meet them. If the objectives of the organisation and information don't match, a 'data gap' has occurred.

Currency

Currency, as stated by DAMA (2009, p.296),[26] can be defined as: 'the degree to which information is current with the world that it models'.

This outlines how up to date the information held by the organisation is over time.

Consistency

Consistency, according to DAMA(2009, p.296),[27] can be outlined as ensuring that data values in one data set are consistent with other values in another data set.

Data needs to be in a consistent state within the CRM platform and between all associated IT systems within the organisation.

A working example would be where sales being registered in the CRM platform are associated with changes occurring in the inventory system.

The data quality framework

We have looked at what is actually meant by data quality, but how do we ensure that the data in the CRM platform meets the required standard and that it will meet the needs of the organisation?

This is where a data quality framework or process can be introduced by the data team to ensure the data is improved and maintained to the standard required.

Based on the 'Virtuous Cycle of Data Quality' outlined in Loshin (2011, pp.17–19), we can refine this model further to arrive at the REFDGIARC (pronounced ref-dee-gee-arc) model of data quality. REFDGIARC stands for:

---

25 English, L.P. (2009), *Information Quality Applied: Best Practices for Improving Business Information, Processes, and Systems*, Chichester, UK: Wiley.
26 *DAMA-Data Management Body of Knowledge* ©.
27 *DAMA-Data Management Body of Knowledge* ©.

- **R**eview and **E**xamine
- **F**ormulate and **D**efine
- **G**enerate and **I**mplement
- **A**ssess and **R**e-evaluate
- **C**ontinuously.

The stages of the REFDGIARC model of data quality (Figure 4) are as follows:

1   Review and examine the data.
2   Formulate and define data quality rules, standards and metrics.
3   Generate and implement business processes and technological solutions to mitigate data issues.
4   Assess and re-evaluate the impact of the implemented solutions on the data to resolve data quality issues.
5   Continuously check that data standards are being achieved and that data requirements are aligned with changing business goals and objectives.

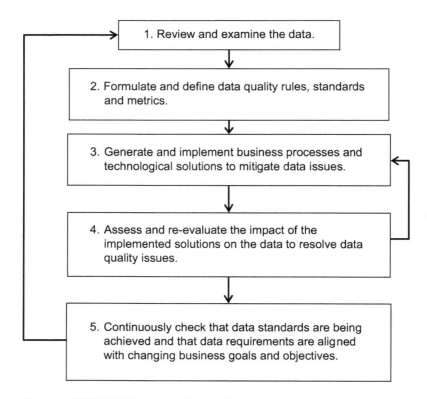

Figure 4 REFDGIARC model of data quality

1. Review and examine the data

Reviewing and examining the data means profiling the data and undertaking an initial assessment of the data quality, which can be part of an audit of the data that is held within the CRM database.

To undertake the data profiling process:

- Specialist data profiling tools can be acquired and deployed.
- Data profiling tools can be developed or computer programs can be written to assess the quality of the data within the organisation.
- Some database platforms have data quality tools that can be used.
- The data profiling process can be undertaken by a third-party data provider.

The data profiling phase will establish and highlight any issues with the data and form the basis for solutions to be implemented in the system.

The data profiling phase can be undertaken by the organisation itself or by an external organisation, depending on the resources available.

The following aspects of data that will be assessed during the data profiling stage are outlined by the DataFlux Corporation (2003, pp.5–12):[28]

- pattern matching – analysing the different patterns of the data; an example would be looking at the different forms in which a country has been input into the CRM platform, such as US or USA;
- domain checking – checking the correct value has been entered into the database field; for example, when dealing with checkboxes, the value can be Y, N, Yes, No – what values are to be used in these contexts?
- range checking – checking that the values of fields in the database are within expected value ranges;
- cross-field verification – comparing values in one field to another to see whether they are valid; using the example of countries and states, if the country is the USA in the country field, are only valid state values being entered into the state field?
- address format verification – ensuring that addresses are correctly formatted; for example, Avenue can be Ave or Avenue;
- name standardisation – ensuring that names of people are standardised within the organisation; for example, Andrew can be called Andy;
- reference field consolidation – checking whether a reference ID used to identify a particular attribute, say an organisation or product type, is unique to that attribute; for example, CS is a product reference category for computer screen products, not computer software;
- format consolidation – ensuring that standardised formats for dates, prices and telephone numbers are used within the CRM platform;

---

28 DataFlux Corporation (2003), *Data Profiling: The Foundation for Data Management* – Copyright © 2004, SAS Institute Inc., Cary, NC, USA. All Rights Reserved. Reproduced with permission of SAS Institute Inc., Cary, NC.

- Referential integrity – ensuring that the data is correctly referenced between tables in the database; for example, details of a particular order number may exist in an orders table of the database, but no record of the products that are attached to that order are linked to that order number in a corresponding table;
- duplicate identification – ensuring that duplicated data is identified, merged or deleted from the CRM platform;
- basic statistics, frequencies, ranges and outliers – basic statistical techniques like mean, mode and median will be used to analyse the data to uncover anomalies and possible data errors;
- uniqueness and missing value validation – looking at values used to identify records uniquely or values that could be missing;
- key identification – making sure that the key to identify a record contact or product is the same key that is used to identify that product in other database systems; for example, if a product has a number 01234, make sure 01234 is the product in your inventory database;
- data rule compliance – testing the data rules that have been applied to the data in the database structure; for example, if a product is out of stock, an order cannot be processed.

2. Formulate and define data quality rules, standards and metrics

The organisation needs to formulate and define baseline and acceptable data quality metrics and data quality rules.

This involves defining in quantifiable terms the quality level and standard that the data held within the CRM platform should be achieving for the organisation to consider that the data is of the required standard to meet organisational objectives.

DAMA (2009, p.299)[29] outlines the following characteristics that could be used by an organisation when setting data quality metrics. These include:

- Measurable – when defining data quality metrics they need to be assessable, but also meaningful to the organisation.
- Business-relevant – the metric needs to be relevant to the organisation's data management operations.
- Acceptability – baseline and acceptable data quality thresholds need to be determined by the business expectations of the organisation.
- Accountability – when data quality levels are below the acceptable level determined by the organisation, corrective action needs to be undertaken. Who within the organisation is responsible for ensuring that data quality is maintained needs to be outlined.
- Controllability – a suitable data quality metric should incorporate some kind of controllability. This means that if data quality falls below the level acceptable to an organisation, some kind of action will be taken to rectify and improve the situation.

29 *DAMA-Data Management Body of Knowledge ©.*

- Trackability – the data quality metrics that are chosen by an organisation need to be measurable over time. This will enable the organisation to discover any issues and problems that may be occurring within the data lifecycle.

Types of data quality metrics

DAMA (2009, p.349)[30] suggests possible areas that can be used as data quality metrics:

a) Data values statistics – this is information about the values that are held within the CRM database. The aspects of the data that would be looked at would include criteria like:

- Are the values in the correct format?
- Are the values within acceptable range limits?
- Should there be any null values in a particular field?

b) Errors/requirement violations – these data quality metrics relate to the number of errors that occurred during a process or task. This area of data metrics should not only be concerned with how many errors occurred, but also the types of errors that are occurring during a process or task. With this information, the organisation can identify potential problem areas and implement solutions where necessary.

c) Conformance to expectations – these data quality metrics outline potential problems when the data quality metrics are below the expectations of the organisation. An example would when introducing a new technology or process into the organisation. The expectation of the organisation is that it will work 99.9% of the time. If the technology or process falls below this threshold, then the issue needs to be fixed, the technology replaced or an alternative solution implemented.

d) Conformance to service levels – these metrics look at the service levels that have been introduced/set by the organisation that are considered to be acceptable regarding an aspect of data quality. Service levels for technology may have already been defined by the manufacturer. When dealing with service level agreements, great care must be taken when defining service levels. For example, it may be that service levels are continuously not being achieved. However, this may not indicate that there could be an issue with data quality. It could be that the service level set by the organisation was completely unrealistic and was not achievable in the first place. When setting service levels within a data team or an organisation, use SMART objectives as a guide. If service levels are not being achieved, investigate and assess why, so that solutions can be implemented to ensure the required standard can be attained. Using DAMA (2009, pp.302–303),[31] when the metrics have been outlined, a data quality matrix grid could be developed (see Figure 5).

---

30 *DAMA-Data Management Body of Knowledge* ©.
31 *DAMA-Data Management Body of Knowledge* ©.

Data quality metric	Target	Actual	Metric test methodology	Testing schedule	Responsibility	Date
Number of duplicates within the database will not exceed 1% of the total number of records within the database at any time.				Weekly, daily monthly etc.		
The number of returns or email bounce-backs from postal or email campaigns is less than 1% of the mailing count.						

Figure 5 Data quality metrics grid

Data quality rules

After the initial profiling stage, the definition and design of the data quality rules need to be established.

Data quality rules can be applied to entities – for example, a contact record as well as individual fields and processes involved in the management of the CRM platform.

Examples of data quality rules include:

- in all new contact records, an email address needs to be mandatory;
- the value entered into the email address field needs to contain the @ symbol.

3. Generate and implement business processes and technological solutions to mitigate data issues

When the data quality rules, data quality standards and metrics have been established, solutions can be generated and implemented to improve data quality.

These are the actual solutions that will be used to improve data quality within the CRM platform.

Using the previous definition of data quality, some possible solutions to improving data quality are outlined below.

Timeliness

Practical measures that can be implemented to ensure data timeliness is achieved include:

a) Schedules and work planners – ensure staff responsible for producing mailings and reports are aware of deadlines and schedules so that work can be organised to meet these target dates.
b) Organising and preparing work – report queries for standard reports and mailings that are needed on a regular basis can be written once then stored to be used at a later date. If your database platform has the functionality to schedule and run reports automatically, then use this feature to reduce workloads.
c) Service level agreements – service level agreements should be introduced for when data will be processed or imported into the database.
d) Automating tasks and processes – Automating workflows could be investigated by the organisation to reduce delays in the availability of data.

These methods may help reduce the 'data lag time' within the organisation. The ideal situation would be that there is no data lag time at all.

Accuracy

To improve the accuracy of the data held on the database, the following systems could be implemented:

a) internal data cleaning – data cleaning and spot checks of information on the CRM database should be undertaken by data team staff.
b) External agencies – data can be checked by external agencies for changes in address, deceased individuals and telephone numbers.
c) Accurate data capture – accurate data capture at source will improve the accuracy and consistency of the data collected.
d) Mailing preference and contact information data files – these can be integrated into the CRM platform or used by a third-party data provider or organisation to clean the data to ensure the accuracy of information in the database such as a contact's mailing preferences and contact details are correct.
e) Data verification tools – data being entered into the CRM platform can be verified in real time by checking the data against data files, for example checking valid addresses are being input into the CRM platform or when information is being entered into an online or electronic form.
f) Scheduling of data cleaning – data cleaning should be scheduled, and what type of cleaning should be undertaken and when it should occur should be defined. Examples of this include using spot checks for data imports undertaken by internal staff. The cleaning of distribution lists should be carried out every month by internal staff. An external agency should check the data every six months. Suppression files should be used before a mailing is sent out by the organisation.

g) Data cleaning queries and tools – computer code or SQL can be written and data cleaning tools can be used and run periodically to keep the data in the database as clean as possible.

h) Service level agreements (SLAs) and key performance indicators (KPIs) – data cleaning could be part of the data team's KPIs or SLA agreements, for example the cleaning of distribution lists within the organisation.

i) Training and support of staff – ensure that staff are trained to enter data into the database correctly. Staff need to be trained how to enter contacts and organisations into the CRM platform correctly, otherwise they may not appear in mailings for specific products, services or informational mailings.

j) Preventing data (record) duplication – measures need to be implemented to prevent duplicate data (records) being created within the CRM platform. Solutions need to incorporate the identification and cleaning (merging) of duplicate data stored in the CRM platform and the suppression of duplicate data being entered or imported into the system. This could mean the development of processes and procedures such as when training staff that an important aspect of data entry is first checking that the data does not already exist on the database before entering data on the system or the implementation of technology to reduce the possibility of duplicates being created within the CRM platform. Some CRM platforms may already have built-in functionality to assist in the recognition and elimination of duplicate data (records).

k) Data matching rules – ensure that the organisation has implemented data matching business rules so that multiple records are not entered into the database.

l) Automating tasks – where possible, tasks should be automated to reduce human error.

m) Data silos – it is important to avoid having data silos, by merging data sets into one data source, for example within the CRM platform, which will improve the information about the organisation's customers and clients.

n) Database design – ensure that related fields and values are correctly referenced and built into the design of the database. For example, if you have a postal city of London, it should only be possible to select only London postcodes in the postcode field.

Completeness

Solutions to ensure that the information held on the CRM platform is considered complete include:

a) Business rules –rules could be imposed in the design of the database to impose constraints on the data. Database fields can be specified as mandatory and required, or optional. You can also define whether values can be null or not null. Default values can be specified when necessary.

b) Using software programs – auto-population software, possibly linked to third-party data sources, could be implemented. It could be used in capturing business and consumer addresses to ensure as much information is complete and accurate as possible.

c) Data enrichment programme – the organisation can implement a data enrichment programme to enhance information already held on the CRM platform so that the organisation can achieve its objectives.
d) Third-party organisations – these may be able to offer data enhancement/ enrichment services to identify information missing from the CRM platform data set.
e) Research programme – this could be initiated by the organisation to find and fill in any missing data gaps within the CRM database data sets.

Relevance

Ensure the information being collected and held on the CRM platform is relevant to the organisation's present and future information needs so that organisational objectives can be achieved.

Any information gaps in the organisational data sets should be filled by research or by buying the necessary data from an external supplier.

The organisation should have a plan for the collection and capture of data so that the organisation's data requirements are being fulfilled.

Currency

To improve the currency of the data within the CRM platform, possible solutions include:

a) Cleaning of data sets – if your information has been segmented into groups and these are used on a regular basis for mailings, then these need to be checked and cleaned.
b) Data cleaning – undertake periodic data cleaning on the information held within the CRM platform.
c) Third-party data – this can be a benefit to an organisation, to complement the data that is already in the system or help fill in any missing information that has been identified. How reliable the third-party data is should also be questioned, asking: 'how do I know the data I'm receiving is good enough for the purpose I need it for?' The following questions also need to be addressed:

- How was the data collected?
- How old is the data?
- When was it checked?

If information obtained from a single data source constantly yields results that do not meet your requirements, then a more reliable data source needs to be found.

The same questions can also be applied to the information that is held within the CRM platform.

Consistency

The following methods and guidelines will help improve the consistency of data within the CRM platform:

a) Systems integration and third-party applications – if third-party applications are used in conjunction with the CRM platform, the data changes in a application needs to match the held in the CRM platform. For example, if a third-party email application is to be used, then bounce-backs from the mailing need to be recorded in the CRM platform so that the data can be cleaned. Other systems in other departments in the organisation may need to be integrated into the CRM platform so that the information is consistent across all departments and systems.

b) Data validation – this is to ensure that values are within specified ranges, in the correct format and that correct data types are entered into the CRM platform. Specific data validation tools can be developed to the check the data before it is imported into the database. Most CRM platforms incorporate some sort of data validation before the data is imported into the database to highlight any data issues such as wrong values. Some CRM platforms allow for the creation of validation rules on fields within the CRM platform to ensure the correct data is entered into the system.

c) Data feeds – ensure that data feeds and ETL (Extract, Transform, Load) processes between various IT systems have been correctly set up and maintained.

d) Drop-down menus – these types of menus will ensure that the data is pre-formatted and only specified values are entered into a field.

e) Input masks – these are used to format the data correctly. Examples of this include the correct formatting of postcodes and dates. The formatting of data is important as it may affect the results of data being queried and retrieved from the database for reporting, analysis and mailings.

f) Merging of various data sources – the data team may be dealing with information from different sources and in different formats. The data needs to be merged into a consistent state and any data anomalies dealt with before it is imported into the database platform.

g) Procedures for dealing with data anomalies – if data anomalies are occurring, procedures for identifying and resolving data errors should be implemented.

h) Data templates – if you are importing data into the database, set up import templates that match fields already in the database. If you are using a CRM platform's import wizard (if it has this functionality), fields on the import template should automatically match the fields in the database for the data to be imported into the database. Import templates should have the same data validation and formatting criteria specified for the database to ensure consistency and reduce import errors. Reporting templates can be developed to ensure a consistent format is used within the organisation and help process reports more efficiently.

i) Program code – this can be used to ensure information is correctly standardised within the database platform and across IT systems within the organisation.

j) Data capture at source – ensure that data collected at source is valid and accurate. When initially collecting data, ensure that:

- the data being captured is valid – for example the data type is correct e.g. text, date etc.;
- the information you require is being collected – for example, email address, postal address;
- the data being collected can be stored within the CRM platform.

k) Third-party suppliers – if these are to be used in data processing, ensure that any changes in the CRM platform are communicated to the data processing supplier so that errors are not continually sent through, wasting time with unnecessary trouble-shooting of problems that should already have been resolved.

l) Implementation of procedures and guidelines on how to use the CRM platform – the way the CRM platform is used within the organisation needs to be consistent across all departments. Procedures and guidelines and staff training will help ensure that the process to complete a task on the CRM platform is the same for all those using it. An organisation may outsource some of it data management and quality responsibilities to a third-party supplier – in these cases, the procedures and processes the service provider has implemented to ensure organisational data quality is maintained while the provider processes the data need to be investigated and reviewed.

Integrating the CRM platform into a website

Websites are used for a variety of reasons, such as ecommerce or communicating with the public, and can be employed to collect information about people interested in an organisation's services, products or causes.

If a website is to be used as a method of collecting and capturing information, data quality measures need to be applied to the Web forms that are used to collect that information. For example, the Web form should have the same data validation and formatting criteria that are specified for the database.

Some CRM platforms may already have their own Web/CRM integration module, allowing data to be collected via a website and imported into the CRM platform directly without the necessity of the additional step of producing an import file to import the data into the database.

These modules help the organisation to collect data from a website in the correct format and adhere to any data validation rules that are applied to any of the fields within the database. These rules could cover:

- correct format of the data – for example, date format 20/12/2012;
- correct value ranges;
- correct values for a field – for example, using a specified county/state, depending on the country.

When developing data capture forms, ensure that they include some form of validation and are consistent with the validation rules used in the CRM platform.

If the organisation does not have templates to produce Web forms for data collection, HTML (Hypertext Markup Language – a computer language used to develop Web pages) includes built-in form validation rules and features.

This, combined with JavaScript (another computer language), will validate that all the information required on the form has been collected and in the correct format before it is incorporated into the organisation's CRM database.

Depending on the CRM platform's functionality, data collected via the Web can be automatically processed (updated or imported) directly or require a member of the data team to check and manually update or import the changes into the CRM platform.

Other considerations when incorporating an organisation's website into its CRM platform include:

- security;
- the process to enable external customers/organisations to view and edit data;
- how the data from the website is to be processed.

4. Assess and re-evaluate the impact of the implemented solutions on the data to resolve data quality issues

After integrating solutions into the CRM platform to mitigate data quality issues, the organisation needs to objectively assess and re-evaluate whether the implemented solution has resolved the problems.

How the organisation verifies that data quality issues have been mitigated will depend on the nature of the issues that need to be resolved and the data standards that have been defined by the organisation (Stage 2 of this framework).

This stage is important, as if the solution introduced to attain the required standards is not effective or data quality rules are not being successfully implemented, the organisation needs to amend, adapt or re-engineer the current solution or implement a new one that resolves specific data issues – for example, repeating Stage 3 of the data quality framework.

5. Continuously check that data standards are being achieved and that data requirements are aligned with changing business goals and objectives

The final phase of the process is continuous monitoring and review of the processes and solutions that have been introduced to improve the quality of the data.

Once data quality targets have been achieved as outlined by the organisation, then the standard needs to be maintained, so a system for monitoring the data needs to be implemented.

DAMA (2009, p.304)[32] sets out the level at which monitoring of the data should occur and how this can be carried out.

Monitoring should occur at three levels of granularity:

- data element;
- data record;
- data set.

32 *DAMA-Data Management Body of Knowledge* ©.

These can be monitored under the following conditions:

a) batch analysis – taking a sample or batch of data which is then analysed;
b) instream analysis – assessing data within a process and when a data set changes from one process to another.

These processes could have some degree of automation, but usually involve someone running scripts to test the quality of the data.

Software tools specialising in data profiling and data quality assessment can also be acquired by the organisation if necessary.

Monitoring needs to be continuous and scheduled into the work that is undertaken on the data.

The monitoring and review phase will:

- ensure that data quality standards are being maintained;
- highlight any problems within the data as it is being added to the CRM platform;
- ensure that solutions implemented in the CRM platform to improve data quality are working; if the solutions are not working, corrective actions can be implemented;
- enable the organisation to review how it defines data quality as its data requirements change;
- ensure that an assessment of how the data is reviewed and monitored is undertaken; test scripts and the monitoring process itself should also be reviewed.

The monitoring process, like the initial data profiling phase, can be undertaken internally by the organisation or by an external organisation.

This in essence is undertaking a gap analysis profile of the data – the difference between expected data quality level and what is actually being achieved.

Up to this point, we have only discussed how the data can be continuously checked and evaluated to ensure data standards are being maintained with an organisation.

Another factor that needs to be checked is that the data requirements are aligned with the organisation's changing requirements.

If the objectives and goals of the business change, then the data standards and requirements need to be aligned to meet these changing requirements.

These potential issues with the data are highlighted by going back to Stage 1 of the data quality framework: review and examine the data.

The stages in the data quality framework can then be repeated, to improve and maintain data quality in the CRM platform.

Case study

For some time, Data XYZ PLC has felt that its data does not meet the requirements of the organisation.

The website that could be used for data capture is not connected to the CRM platform.

Web forms that are used to capture information have no form validation and do not match the values in the CRM platform. This causes errors when importing the data into the database, extending the time it takes to process the data.

The CRM platform has little data validation, leading to errors in data entry when data is processed internally.

When importing data, there are no checks for duplication and the formatting of the data, which means that multiple instances of the same contact are being imported into the CRM database.

Data files from sales staff are being imported into the database without questions being asked about where the data originated from.

Data being processed from third-party data suppliers is being imported into the database with no checks, and data files suffer from common errors that are not being addressed by the organisation.

The CRM platform is not integrated with other internal systems.

The email system used for mailings is not synchronised with the CRM platform, so bounce-backs from email campaigns are not being cleaned within the records contained in the CRM platform.

Sales staff are not updating records within a reasonable timeframe. They are creating data silos of contacts that reside in spreadsheet format on their personal computer hard drives. This is causing problems in defining a single view of a customer, and indeed impeding finance staff establishing the exact status of the company in financial terms.

SLAs do not exist within the data team for the processing of data, leading to problems and a question mark over how reliable any reports being generated from the CRM platform are.

Documentation on work processes between the data team and internal company departments does not exist.

There seems to be no training programme for new members of staff in the use of the CRM platform.

Possible improvements in this case study scenario

The following measures will help to improve the quality of the data that is captured by the organisation.

As much as possible, data needs to be cleaned, formatted and checked at source in order to prevent data quality issues and problems developing within the CRM platform. This will also reduce the necessity of the organisation to introduce data quality solutions to mitigate and resolve data issues while it is being processed.

Validation rules need to be implemented on the website forms and within the CRM platform to only allow the correct values to be captured and entered into the CRM database. Auto-population software could be used for the completion of fields and to validate contact information.

Data being processed by third-party suppliers that is to be imported into the CRM platform needs to be examined. Data validation tools can be used to check for duplicate records, validation rules and data quality rule compliance, and other data anomalies before the data is imported into the CRM platform.

Third-party data suppliers need to be kept informed of any data processing errors that are occurring so that these can be addressed before files are sent to Data XYZ PLC.

If third-party data is bought by the organisation, the data should be evaluated in terms of quality and any legal issues addressed before data files are consolidated into the CRM platform.

The practice of importing data files into the CRM platform from sales staff without knowing where they originated from needs to be stopped due to potential legal issues surrounding the data.

The website and third-party systems need to be integrated with the CRM platform. This will:

- reduce the chance of data duplication, inputting incorrect values into the CRM system and data inaccuracies on various systems, such as different email addresses occurring on the email and CRM platform;
- provide a single view of a customer;
- help distribute relevant information to relevant parties within the organisation;
- help to update the data in a timely manner;
- allow details from the website to be automatically updated or imported into the database after the data has been verified and checked by a member of the data team.

A comprehensive cleaning programme should be introduced by the data team. This will comprise a combination of using an outside data cleaning provider and internal data cleaning programs.

Sales staff must stop creating data silos for legal/security and data quality reasons, and must ensure that the information on the CRM platform is as accurate and up to date as possible. If necessary, the data team could provide support to the sales team in processing the data.

SLAs for the data team should be implemented to cover how it processes data. This will improve the validity and reliability of any reports that are generated from the CRM platform.

Workflows, procedures, schedules and guidelines should be implemented and documented so that the data team and other departments can maximise efficiency while the data and work are kept to the required standard.

This should be underpinned by the introduction of a comprehensive training programme for employees who need to use the CRM platform.

Training should be made mandatory as part of the induction process for new employees.

Training programmes should be developed so that training geared to different user skill levels – beginner, intermediate or advanced – can be requested at any time.

A data audit should be undertaken by the data team to see what data is on the system and how it can be improved. This will form the basis of future plans to improve the quality of the data.

The implementation of a data capture process and strategy is suggested so that the organisation's data requirements are geared to achieving future business objectives.

Summary

The organisation needs to implement a data capture (collection) process and strategy that will answer the following questions:

- How is the data to be collected?
- What data is to be collected?
- Where is this data going to come from?
- What technology will be used to store the information – for example, a CRM platform?

Data quality is a multifaceted term. Its definition could include:

- timeliness;
- currency;
- accuracy;
- relevance;
- consistency;
- completeness.

The goal is to ensure that an organisation's data is of a high quality and meets the requirements of the organisation though an ongoing process that involves everyone who uses the CRM platform.

The benefits of having data that is of a high quality include:

- improved decision-making at senior management level;
- improved reporting and analysis within the organisation;
- better understanding, targeting and identification of customers within the organisation's business environment;
- reducing costs through improved efficiency with the introduction of effective data workflows throughout the organisation.

A data quality framework and process need to be implemented within the organisation to improve data quality within the CRM platform so that it is able to help the organisation to achieve its objectives.

The REFDGIARC data quality model stands for:

- **R**eview and **E**xamine
- **F**ormulate and **D**efine
- **G**enerate and **I**mplement

- Assess and **R**e-evaluate
- **C**ontinuously.

The stages of the REFDGIARC model of data quality are as follows:

1 Review and examine the data.
2 Formulate and define data quality rules, standards and metrics.
3 Generate and implement business processes and technological solutions to mitigate data issues.
4 Assess and re-evaluate the impact of the implemented solutions on the data to resolve data quality issues.
5 Continuously check that data standards are being achieved and that data requirements are aligned with changing business goals and objectives.

DAMA (2009, p.312)[33] outlined the following principles for the sort of guidelines that could be introduced into a data quality programme within an organisation:

- Manage data as core organisational asset. Many organisations even place the data as an asset on their balance sheet.
- All data elements will have a standardised data definition, data type and acceptable domain value.
- Leverage data governance for the control and performance of the data quality programme.
- Downstream data consumers specify data quality expectations.
- Define business rules to assert conformance to data quality expectations.
- Business process owners will agree to and abide by data quality service level agreements.
- Apply data corrections at source if possible.
- If it is not possible to correct data at source, forward data corrections to the original owner of the source. Where possible when dealing with data brokers and third-party providers, try to make them conform to the data requirements of the organisation.
- Identify a gold record for all data elements.
- Report measured levels of data quality to appropriate data stewards, business process owners and service level managers.

Data quality is not just an issue for the data team looking after and maintaining the CRM platform. Data quality should be viewed as an organisation-wide issue, and programmes and solutions to improve data quality should be implemented throughout the organisation and be considered an ongoing process.

A CRM database is only as good as the data it holds.

33 *DAMA-Data Management Body of Knowledge* ©.

MANAGEMENT AND ORGANISATION OF THE DATA TEAM

This section will cover:

- how a data team is located within the organisational structure;
- the different roles and responsibilities within a data team;
- management issues of the data team, including effective leadership, developing effective teams, analysing team performance, and selecting the right people for the team.

When the CRM platform has been designed and implemented in the organisation, it needs to be managed, administered and continually developed to meet the organisation's needs.

The organisation needs to have in place structures and systems in place so that:

- tasks on the CRM platform can be carried out as effectively and efficiently as possible;
- members of staff responsible for the CRM platform are able to meet the ever-changing workloads and demands that are going to be placed on the CRM platform;
- effective workflows and processes exist between the data team, external suppliers and internal departments.

This will entail:

- identifying who is responsible for the CRM platform within the organisation;
- defining what tasks they are responsible for undertaking regarding the CRM platform;
- positioning the CRM platform within the organisation so that it is used effectively.

This will help decide how people within the organisation are going to be organised and structured so that they are able to administer the CRM database effectively.

Data team structure

Even though there are other factors that may determine how a team is organised, most data teams organise themselves depending on what functions and responsibilities they are expected to carry out to support the organisation in meeting its objectives.

The tasks that will be undertaken by the CRM data team need to be defined. Core administration tasks that will more than likely be undertaken by the CRM data team include:

- importing data;
- user training and support;
- database development and testing;

- assisting in the compiling of mailing lists;
- data cleaning tasks.

Additional tasks will depend upon the type of organisation, the roles and responsibilities of staff, and the workflows that have been implemented within the organisation to undertake data tasks in the most efficient way possible. They may include:

- reporting and analysis;
- processing information;
- undertaking data audits;
- assisting in developing data strategies and plans.

Here is an outline of how data tasks could be organised within an organisation.

Most of the data processing will be undertaken by sales staff – updating records and notes etc.

Analysts within the marketing team will analyse the data to identify new target segments and report on the progress of the sales team.

The data team may fulfil a support function, managing and maintaining the data and supporting staff members in carrying out their work.

Alternatively, data processing and reporting/analysis could be undertaken by staff within the data team themselves.

The structure of the data team could be organised around these different tasks that need to be carried out for the organisation to achieve its business goals and objectives.

Figure 6 shows a suggestion for a simple organisational structure for a data team, taking account of the responsibilities the team will be expected to carry out within the organisation. The database manager and administrators are responsible for undertaking the daily tasks of upkeep and maintenance of the CRM database with the support of other data team members who are responsible for tasks like reporting and analysing the data.

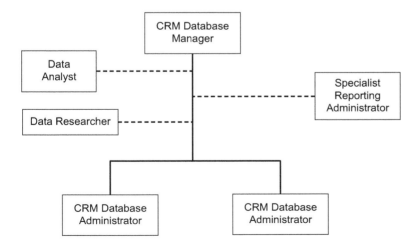

Figure 6 A simple data team organisational structure

What is important is that the team is organised and structured so that it can process the data in the most efficient way so that the organisation can meet its objectives.

Due to the amount of data it has to manage, an organisation may need teams of people to undertake the various tasks within the data department, such as importing/exporting data, reporting etc.

The tasks that are to be undertaken by the data team centrally and those that are to be undertaken by other teams within the business should be defined and taken into consideration when designing the CRM platform.

Positioning of the CRM team within the organisation

As stated earlier, the size and composition of the data team will vary depending on the organisation and the roles and responsibilities the data team is expected to undertake.

Indeed, the data team may be one part of a wider data or business function/ department.

Positioning of the CRM team within the organisation is concerned with where in the organisational structure the data team will be situated to effectively carry out the tasks it is responsible for while being able to meet the demands of the organisation in the most effective way possible.

The most obvious place for the CRM team to be situated within the organisation would be the marketing department, due to the nature of the tasks the CRM team will be undertaking. However, CRM database teams are sometimes located in operational/support services departments. This may offer the advantage that the CRM data team can more easily support the needs of other departments and staff within the organisation that rely on the CRM platform for some aspects of their work.

The data team could be a support function all on its own – for example, reporting, analysis, data processing etc. – so that it able to meet the needs of the various departments within the organisation.

Once the positioning of the data team within the organisational structure has been agreed, procedures, guidelines and workflows can be implemented to govern how the data team is to work with other teams and departments in the organisation.

Workflows, guidelines, procedures and processes for the CRM team

Workflows

Workflows need to be implemented within the organisation so that:

- the responsibilities of teams and team members within the organisation are clearly defined;
- organisation staff are aware of the processes that have been implemented for activities like reporting and mailings;
- data and data tasks are processed in the most efficient and effective way possible.

Some database platforms come with workflow functionality already built in. This enables any work to be approved, checked or verified before it goes on to the next stage of the process.

Some database platforms also come with the functionality to set up data tasks within the database platform to be processed by the data team, which enables work to be monitored.

When setting up workflows within a CRM platform, it's important to ensure that:

- the workflows represent the business processes within the organisation;
- processes are well researched and documented before implementing them within the CRM platform;
- processes reflect the changing circumstances of the organisation – for example, a change in personnel and organisational structure.

If workflows are not part of the functionality of the database platform, other existing IT systems can be used to implement workflows within the data team and organisation. A simple example could be using an email application to set up a centralised email account for any data queries to be sent to the data team to be processed. The email account could be accessed by all members of the data team and the work could be easily monitored.

Guidelines, procedures and processes

Guidelines, procedures and processes formalise:

- how individual tasks are to be undertaken using the CRM platform, such as updating data;
- the identification of different stages that need to be systematically worked through, which may be undertaken departmentally or interdepartmentally to complete a data task, such as how a mailing is produced;
- the allocation of responsibilities, authority and accountability within the organisation and among individuals and third-party providers who are involved in the data processes of the organisation.

This will help the organisation to answer the questions:

- Who is responsible for what tasks?
- When are these tasks to be undertaken?
- How are these tasks to be carried out?

The setting up of these guidelines and procedures should begin with the identification of:

- what tasks are undertaken by individuals using the CRM Platform;
- who is responsible for carrying out these tasks;
- the workflows within the organisation at a team, departmental and interdepartmental level.

Formal guidelines and procedures can then be written and established, and should be reviewed regularly and updated accordingly. Any changes to these guidelines and procedures needs to be communicated to the relevant team members or department.

Regardless of what final solutions are implemented within the organisation, business and data workflows and practices need to be identified and mapped within the data team and within the wider department and organisation to ensure that not only is the work effectively processed, but the data is used to its full potential.

Management of the CRM data team

Management style

The management style adopted by a CRM data manager may be influenced by factors such as the type of individual the manager is, the organisational culture the team operates within and the size of the team, to name but a few.

In broad terms, there are four main management styles that can be adopted by a manager:

a) Autocratic – an autocratic leader determines who will be carrying out what work, how the work will done, and when it is to be completed by. There is no discussion with team members. How the task is to be completed is left at the discretion of the leader, and no one else.

b) Democratic – a democratic style of leadership involves the leader engaging with the team on how tasks are carried out and who will be undertaking them. An example of this is having regular team meetings to outline what needs to be done and who will be undertaking certain tasks. The person carrying out a task is given the opportunity and responsibility for making sure that it is completed.

c) Situational – a situational approach is when the style of the leadership is determined by the task and work that need to be completed by the team. An example of this could be if a task needs to be achieved at short notice or some task unexpectedly needs to be completed that falls outside the team's business-as-usual routine. In order for that task to be completed by a specific deadline, the leader may adopt a more autocratic approach, outlining what needs to be done, who will be doing what, and when it will be completed by. After this situation has passed, the leader may revert to a more democratic style of leadership.

d) Laissez-faire – a laissez-faire leadership style is when a leader decides not to proactively engage with the team and adopts a hands-off, leave the team to get on with it approach.

Motivation and engaging members of staff

Motivating the team

An important aspect of being a leader is the ability to motivate and ensure that team members are engaged with the work they are responsible for.

Motivation can be defined as stated by Worsam (2002, p.140):[34] 'An affective conative factor which operates in determining the direction of an individual's behaviour towards an end or goal, consciously apprehended, or unconscious (*Dictionary of Psychology*)'.

There are broadly two approaches a manager could use to motivate staff.

FINANCIAL REWARDS

Financial rewards can be used to motivate team members and staff. They can be used to improve productivity, but also as a way of engaging team members with the work being carried out and the organisation they work for.

Examples of how financial incentives could work in a data environment include the following:

a) A data processing role salary may be partly based on how much data a person can input. The more data a person can enter accurately onto the CRM platform, the higher the bonus that person will receive.
b) A person may receive a financial reward for coming up with an idea that saves the organisation money or improves work processes. Data staff should have a basic salary that reflects not only their roles and experience, but also the responsibility of being the main custodians of the data held by the organisation.

NON-FINANCIAL REWARDS

Non-financial rewards could include:

a) recognising good work – for example, an employee of the month scheme or complimenting someone on a piece of work that has been carried out beyond expectations;
b) giving staff more responsibility – trusting staff with more important tasks to undertake or increasing their role responsibilities;
c) developing staff – sending staff on courses so that they can improve their skills and the team can better meet the demands of the organisation.

To summarise: it's no good for an organisation to say 'We value consumers' if the staff looking after the data don't feel valued themselves.

What incentive is there for staff to be motivated to take responsibility for being the main custodians of customer data held by the organisation and be willing to accept the consequences that may occur for the organisation if their work is incorrectly carried out if the organisation doesn't look after them?

---

34 Worsam, M. (2002), *Effective Management for Marketing*, Oxford: Butterworth-Heinemann, p.140.

Some ways for managers to help motivate staff were set out by Phipps and Simmons (2002, p.90):[35]

- Get to know them.
- Help them achieve success.
- Give them a feeling of control over their work.
- Build their self-esteem.

METHODS OF ENGAGING STAFF

Work methodologies that could be used to improve work engagement and improve staff motivation, as stated by Worsam (2002, p.162),[36] include:

a) Job enlargement – this can involve giving a team member more tasks to undertake in addition to their original job description.

   This could be used as an opportunity for the staff member to take more responsibly for the work being carried out.

   An example of job enlargement would be that a member of staff is tasked with processing data into the database. The job could be extended to providing reporting and analysis of the work carried out. This method could be used to develop a team member's knowledge and abilities and provide the opportunity to learn new skills while contributing to dealing with the data team's workload.

b) Job rotation – this is the rotation of tasks within the data team. This could be effectively used if you have boring and monotonous tasks that need to be undertaken regularly – 'business as usual' tasks.

   It can also give the opportunity for team members to use their full skill set and start to learn and develop new abilities.

   This method can be effective in training new members of staff so that they get to learn about the different tasks that are undertaken by the data team, why the tasks are carried out, and understand their role within the team.

c) Job enrichment – this can be seen as giving the members within the team more responsibility for the work they are responsible for carrying out.

   Team members are not only given responsibility for carry out a specific task within a process, but are given responsibility for the entire process.

d) Job design – this involves matching the job or role in a team or organisation with the right individual, who will be motivated enough to undertake and carry out that role or job.

   The main point to remember is that 'different jobs require different skills and different personalities', as stated by Worsam (2002, p.162).[37]

35 Phipps, R. and Simmons, C. (2002), *The Marketing Customer Interface*, Oxford: Butterworth-Heinemann, p.90.
36 Worsam, M. (2002), *Effective Management for Marketing*, Oxford: Butterworth-Heinemann, p.162.
37 Worsam, M. (2002), *Effective Management for Marketing*, Oxford: Butterworth-Heinemann, p.162.

Management skills and abilities of the manager

The abilities and skills needed to be a successful manager will probably be a combination of both interpersonal skills and technical abilities.

Interpersonal skills

Interpersonal skills that are needed to be a successful manager would include:

Communication skills

Communication skills and abilities will be essential if the CRM platform is going to be a success.

If the CRM platform is at the centre of any business, the data team will not be isolated from the organisation, but will deal and talk with a variety of staff and outside agencies, and there will be a need to form good working relationships so that the CRM platform can help achieve organisational objectives.

The following methods and guidelines can be employed to help achieve and form these working relationships:

a) It is important to have a good communication network between departments that are responsible for looking after the CRM database, for example the IT department and marketing/third-party providers. Hold regular meetings on how to develop the database/solve issues/develop plans.

 This is also important for contingency planning and to ensure that you have a clear plan when the worst situations occur –data loss, security breaches etc.

b) Set up a working group to develop the database, consisting of stakeholders within the organisation to champion the development of the database – for example, IT and marketing.

 Members of staff can channel their feedback to the working group so that the CRM database can be continually developed to meet the needs of the organisation.

c) Hold regular team meetings to discuss upcoming tasks and priorities, problems that have occurred and need to be resolved, and to provide a forum for team members to discuss any related data topics.

d) Use online media to promote the work of the CRM data team. This could mean using the organisation's intranet to promote the development of the CRM platform.

 Other information that could be included on the intranet could be best practice tips, news of training events, support material, and news of meetings and seminars regarding the CRM platform. A regular newsletter can be used to inform, educate and promote the CRM platform throughout the organisation.

e) Ensure that the database team and wider staff members have access to CRM documentation. These documents could be guidelines and procedures or describe how to undertake a task on the database, or explain where a person can find a data confidentiality form that needs to be signed by all staff when joining the organisation.

Staff should be made aware of where they can locate the relevant documentation, and this information could be part of the staff induction pack.

Documenting the CRM database is important as it:

• underpins the training programme staff should receive on the CRM database;
• assists in maintaining the quality of the information stored in the database;
• outlines where help and support regarding the CRM database can be found;
• instils an ethos of responsibility and best practice for the data staff and outlines how the data should be treated and used within the organisation.
• outlines staff members' roles and responsibilities and the relationships between them and the CRM team.
• improves business continuity and forms a basis for dealing with any changes within the organisation should there be any changes in personnel or structure.

This documentation needs to be reviewed on a regular basis, and if necessary, alterations made so that effective business/working relationships and data workflows within the data team and in its relationships with the wider organisation are maintained and continually improved.

These factors not only help support the members in the data team to do their jobs correctly, but ensure that wider staff members within the organisation are aware of their responsibilities and how they should be operating the CRM platform, ensuring the data is maintained correctly and assisting in meeting wider organisational objectives.

With all these methods of communication, it is important that the manager is able to communicate with a wide variety of audiences inside and outside the organisation.

Not only the manager, but also the CRM data team will be dealing with staff at all levels in all departments within the organisation, and possibly communicating with outside agencies and people.

The CRM data team is providing a service to the organisation, and these interactions reflect on the image people have of the data team and possibly the organisation its members work for.

It is also important that the correct method of communication is chosen depending on the audience and what you are trying to communicate.

Planning

The ability to plan and schedule work is an important to skill for a manager

Tasks need to be planned, prioritised and scheduled in order for deadlines to be achieved while ensuring that the data team is still able to carry out its day-to-day activities.

The ability of the team and how the team and manager react to unexpected events, problems, and ad hoc data tasks that need to be carried out at short notice will also need to be a considered by any manager.

Organisational skills

These entail organising not only staff within the data team, but also any resources that are needed by the team to undertake its work. This may include making sure that staff have access to the software needed to carry out their work. It may also include organising work so that it is efficiently and effectively processed.

An example could be where a member of the data team needs to run a lot of queries for reporting, analysis or for compiling mailings. It may be more efficient to run these queries during a specific time of the day when network usage is low, so that the work can be completed a lot quicker. Other tasks and work can be organised around these optimal processing times to ensure that team members are working as effectively as possible.

Time management skills

These cover the ability to manage not only your own personal time, but the time of the data team members.

System and technical skills

Another important skill set that is required by the data team and manager is the ability to understand and carry out the technical requirements of the job

The system and technical skills needed by a member of the data team will largely depend on their role. For example, the technical skills required by a data analyst will be completely different to those of someone in the data team who is undertaking a data processing function.

From a manager's perspective, it is important to understand the roles and tasks that are undertaken by the team members in order to make effective decisions and co-ordinate the data team as efficiently as possible.

Generally speaking, the technical skills required by the data team centre around the tasks that need to be undertaken on the CRM platform. These include:

- generating reports;
- querying and retrieving information from the database;
- importing and exporting data;
- undertaking data cleaning tasks.

For this task list, the technical skill requirements could include:

- knowledge of SQL (the language used to retrieve information from the database);
- understanding how databases are designed and how information is related within a database;
- how to use third-party data cleaning/profiling/quality management tools;
- how to use third-party reporting software;
- how to use applications like spreadsheets and desktop database programs;
- CRM administration certification to ensure that staff are able to use the CRM platform properly and maximise its full potential.

Data management skills

Data management skills and the knowledge that managers and data team members need include:

- how to maintain and improve data quality;
- data security;
- data governance;
- data legislation.

System and data management skills reviewed

It is important to emphasise that system skills and data management skills are equally important, and both are needed in order to effectively manage the CRM database.

To highlight this point, let's focus on the quality of data within the database.

To improve the data quality within the CRM database, the manager needs a technical understanding of the CRM platform so that solutions can be developed and integrated into the system (technical abilities). The CRM database manager also needs to be able to oversee the entire data quality process and framework so that the data quality standards are being achieved to enable the organisation to achieve its objectives (data management skills).

This shows how system and data management skills are linked and complement one another, and why CRM database managers need both technical and data management abilities if they are to manage a CRM platform successfully.

Responsibilities of the CRM database manager

As well as the day-to-day organisation, planning and management of the CRM database, additional responsibilities of the CRM manager may include the following.

Financial management

The CRM database manager will be expected to be responsible for any financial aspects within the data team. Some of these areas may include:

- developing and maintaining the budget for the data team, to ensure sufficient financial resources have been allocated to carry out the work the team is responsible for;
- keeping a record of financial resources (costs) allocated for projects, suppliers and resources brought into the team to carry out the data work;
- measuring the performance of the data team in financial terms to secure budget allocation and financial resources in the future.

Human resource management

Human resource management is concerned with the management of staff within the data team. Areas the CRM database manager could be responsible for include:

- staff training and development;
- selecting and recruiting staff;
- motivating the team;
- assessing the performance of the team and individual team members.

Some of the aspects of human resource management the database manager will be responsible are discussed below.

Training

The type of training needed for data staff will depend on the roles and tasks they will be responsible for within the team. Various training methods can be used in a variety of situations to develop team members.

Internal training can be used to develop technical skills, and database tasks can be learned when various project work needs to be completed, or it can be as simple as providing on-the-job training. This will increase staff members' knowledge of the CRM platform and widen the scope of work they can undertake.

The use of various types of databases can be included in the training.

An organisation may have a test database for trialling new development features of the CRM platform before they implemented into the live environment. It may also have a training database that can be used to train any member of staff within the organisation without the fear of contaminating the data in the live database environment.

Internal training can be supplemented by external training by sending staff on courses relevant to their roles and areas of responsibility. General courses that all team members could undertake include data management and system certification training courses.

This highlights the need to identify:

- core skills and training necessary for all data team members;
- specific skills and training needed by team members to undertake their roles.

Training guidelines for staff can be developed to keep skills up to date and ensure that team members' skills can meet present and future demands placed on the data team. These may include:

- any mandatory courses staff and data team members need to complete;
- any certifications staff need to achieve.

When any training is required, formalised training plans can be developed in partnership with members of staff as part of the appraisal process.

The aim of the staff development and training process is to foster an environment of continuous learning and improvement so that the needs of the organisation are achieved while staff are able to meet their own goals and objectives.

Recruiting staff

One of the responsibilities of the CRM database manager will be selecting and recruiting staff. The process adopted for this will depend upon some of the following factors:

- the role to be filled;
- organisational culture and industry type;
- the type of position – for example, permanent, temporary or a contract;
- the finances and time available to the organisation to fill the position.

The main stages in the recruitment process are broadly:

a) defining and outlining the role;
b) advertising and finding potential candidates to fill the position;
c) selecting and filling the role.

A) DEFINING AND OUTLINING THE ROLE

This stage involves drawing up a job description for the position that is being filled within the data team.

The job description is a formal statement or criteria list of the tasks, responsibilities, skills and abilities required for a candidate to successfully carry out the role that has been identified as necessary for the data team to meet its goals.

The job description may include the following information:

- job title;
- department/team;
- salary range;
- line manager;
- line management responsibilities;
- description of the role/organisation;
- type of employment;
- commencement date/period of employment;
- skills/abilities needed to carry out the role; these should be defined in two categories – essentials and desirables.
- person specification;
- qualifications.

Here are some points to remember when defining the job description:

It should be as complete as possible – this enables potential candidates to decide whether to apply for the role and ensures that the organisation has a criteria for the selection of candidates.

A statement like 'intermediate spreadsheet/database skills' is not a well-defined skill attribute, whereas 'the candidate must be able to query and retrieve information from a database' is. A well-defined skill attribute will save you time in processing applications from unsuitable candidates.

Keywords in the job description – these need to be included so that recruiters can search for them on their candidate databases and potential candidates can find the role easily when searching on job boards on the Web.

Tasks and responsibilities – tasks that are to be carried out by the successful candidate are a reflection of the current and possible future needs of the data team.

Feedback and review about the job specification – don't be afraid to ask data team members to look at the job specification to see whether other points need to be included in the role, as your decision in hiring someone will have an impact on them as well.

Depending on the type of role being filled, other documentation included with the job description may include:

- equal opportunities policies;
- method of applying for the role – for example, a written application form;
- terms and conditions;
- information about the organisation;
- the schedule for the recruitment process, including the interview and start date;
- confidentiality statements.

B) ADVERTISING AND FINDING POTENTIAL CANDIDATES TO FILL THE POSITION

A variety of methods can be employed to find potential candidates, including:

- recruitment agencies;
- job websites;
- the company website;
- magazines, newspapers etc.;
- promoting the role internally;
- word of mouth.

The role to be filled should be promoted and advertised where the organisation feels suitable candidates may be found.

C) SELECTING AND FILLING THE ROLE

When potential candidates have been found based on the job description, the process of selecting the individual to fill the role can begin.

The methods of selection chosen by the organisation may include one or both of the following:

- interview process;
- testing the potential candidates.

Interview process   The interview process will vary from organisation to organisation, depending on factors such as:

- the position they are trying to fill;
- the type of role (temporary or permanent);
- organisational human resource guidelines and procedures.

These factors in turn will influence the interview process in terms of how many stages it will comprise, types of interview and who will conduct them.

An example of a type of interview used when filling data roles is the competence-based interview, where the candidate is asked a series of questions based on the job specification and abilities needed to carry out the role. These questions might include:

Can you give me an example of when you were part of a team working towards an objective? What was your role? How did you make sure you achieved the objective?

Can you give an example when you provided outstanding customer service?

The interview process should be an opportunity for a candidate to highlight skills and capabilities while the organisation judges whether this is the right person for the role.

It should also be remembered that this is an opportunity for the organisation to get to know the candidate, but also an opportunity for the candidate to get to know the organisation, to see whether they can work together.

Testing a candidate's suitability for the role   In addition to an interview, potential candidates may be required to undergo some kind of tests to evaluate their suitability for the position. These may include:

- personality tests;
- psychometric tests;
- group- or team-based evaluations.

Task/system tests are commonly used when filling data roles, including:

a) Data entry/processing tests – these are used to gauge a candidate's ability to process and enter data quickly and accurately.
b) Computer language tests – these test knowledge of SQL (the language used to retrieve information from the database) or another computer language necessary to undertake the role. They can take the form of:

- answering questions about the computer language;
- writing code in work-based examples which is then assessed by the organisation to determine the candidate's level of proficiency.

c) Data analysis and reporting – depending on the role, the candidate may be asked to undertake some kind of analysis, then report on the findings.
d) Data quality checking tasks – the candidate may be given a sample of data and asked to make suggestions and highlight possible problems within the sample. Depending on the how the test is organised and what is required within the role, the candidate may also be asked to reformat the data. This will test the candidate's system skills as well. These tasks reveal the attention to detail the candidate is capable of and the ability to make suggestions to maintain and improve the quality of the data within the database.
e) System skills – this involves testing candidates on various computer applications to determine whether they have the necessary proficiency to undertake the role. It may include being tested on computer applications like spreadsheets and desktop database applications. It may also include the ability to

use a specific CRM platform. This area of testing should be a continuation of what has already been outlined in the skills and abilities section of the job description. If you are looking for someone who needs to be able to query databases, then these tests should form the basis for your selection process. The types of tests employed by the organisation will depend on:

- the tasks to be undertaken by the successful candidate;
- the system skills and abilities needed to carry out the role.

Examples of systems skill testing in regard to a CRM platform include:

- answering written or verbal questions about the functions and features of the CRM platform;
- practical testing regarding the features and functionality of the CRM platform – for example, how to run a report, how to import data;
- written or practical case studies/work scenarios developed and employed to gain an understanding of candidates' knowledge of the CRM platform, thought processes and work methodology in resolving work-based problems they are likely to encounter in the role they are applying for.

Here are some points to remember when testing candidates:

a) Data – don't use actual client, customer, donor or live information.
b) Use a test environment – don't test people in the live/production version of the CRM database. If testing CRM platform abilities, use a test database or set up a sandbox (a place to test code and try out new features and practice new skills).
c) Provide an objective way to make a decision – the tests should be designed so that you are able to make an objective choice on the potential candidates to fill the role based on what tasks they will be expected to carry out. The tests should also provide an opportunity for candidates to demonstrate their abilities. They should therefore be based on the skills and abilities outlined in the job description.

When the testing and interview process has been completed, the organisation should be able to come to a decision about whether it is able to fill the role. In some circumstances, it may not feel that the right person has been found. In this situation, there are several options:

- don't fill the position, and re-advertise for new candidates;
- put the position on hold, and advertise it again at a later date;
- outsource the task of filling the position to a third-party provider;
- if the organisation is not sure about a candidate, it may be possible to offer a temp-perm position; this provides a further opportunity to evaluate the candidate on the job, and the organisation will benefit from having someone to carry out the required work.

A candidate may not have the exact skills you are looking for, but may have relevant experience that will make it easier to provide cross-training to carry out the work required so that you can offer them the role.

An example of this would be where a candidate does not have experience in a particular CRM database platform but has used other similar platforms. As all CRM platforms have similar functionality and features, the candidate's experience will make it easier for the organisation to provide platform-specific training.

Effective team performance

All the aspects we have discussed so far have been about creating an effective working team environment for tasks to be undertaken so that organisation can achieve its goals.

The performance of the individual and the team needs to be assessed in order to gauge how well they are functioning. The following assessment methods can be used:

a) Reviews – these could be group or individual reviews. They can be held informally on a weekly basis or be part of a more formal review process of another HR function, such as appraisals.

b) Feedback – feedback can be sought from departments and people within and outside the organisation who have interacted with the individual and team while processing data work. Problems encountered when carrying out the work and comments from interested parties should be taken into consideration when measuring team performance.

c) Set targets and objectives – team performance can be measured against set objectives and targets. These could include:

- defined service level agreements for undertaking work as a team and individual;
- working objectives such as what work needs to be completed in a specified time period; these could include: the implementation of different CRM projects within the organisation or personal development targets for individuals within the team – for example, 'I will get this qualification within a certain time period.'

Measuring and evaluating performance is an important part of the management process. It should motivate staff in their work, but also helps to identify areas for personal development and recognises the standard of work within the data team. This can be promoted within the organisation in order to gain the necessary resources for future plans and projects.

Case study

Data XYZ PLC has had a few problems when it comes to staff and management of its CRM platform.

The organisation has experienced high staff turnover in the administrator position for the CRM platform.

In the current organisational structure (see Figure 1 in Chapter 1), the CRM database is located in the business development section of the marketing department. The line manager, who is the business development officer, has no experience of managing a CRM platform and has no technical or managerial knowledge of how to administer a CRM database.

The manager seems to have no interest in the management of the CRM platform and has adopted a laissez-faire attitude to the management of the CRM database, with the CRM administrator taking all the responsibility for how the system is operated with little input from the line manager, who is taking no interest in the CRM administrator's work.

The line manager only works three days a week, and the CRM administrator is expected to undertake all tasks relating to the CRM platform. These include data cleaning, developing the database to meet future organisational needs, reporting, compiling mailings and providing analysis of the data in the database and any campaigns undertaken by the organisation.

This has led to staff who have taken on the role feeling frustrated, demoralised, overworked, undervalued and demotivated, and ultimately leaving the position.

There is little in the way of working processes, procedures and workflows between the teams in the marketing department and internal departments, which is leading to missed deadlines for reporting and mailings.

The culture within the department is one of always looking at the bottom line, and not of adding value to the organisation to move it forward.

The organisation has tried to solve the problem by employing temporary members of staff, but due to lack of training, documentation and support, the position is constantly being vacated.

Possible improvements in this case study scenario

For the department and the organisation to be more productive, the following changes could be implemented.

The data team needs a proper CRM database manager – someone who has the right technical and interpersonal skills who can manage the CRM platform and derive real value from the data, and improve efficiency and workflows in the marketing department and throughout the organisation.

The CRM database manager should also be able to support and assist the CRM administrator where necessary.

The data team needs to be an independent function within the marketing department so that it can fulfil the needs of the different departmental teams and also liaise with other departments to develop the system throughout the entire organisation.

A new structure is suggested in Figure 7.

The specific responsibilities the data team will be undertaking on behalf of the organisation need to be defined and outlined.

When hiring new members of staff, even temporary ones, formal job descriptions should be written for their roles. These should include any system skills, experience, interpersonal skills and knowledge required.

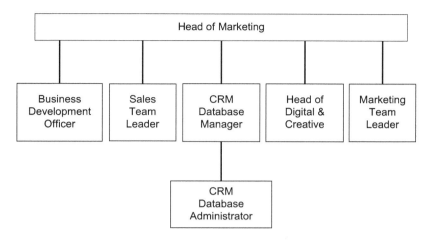

Figure 7 Proposed new marketing department structure of Data XYZ PLC

A formal interview process should be combined with tests on specific skill requirements, such as attention to detail, knowledge of the CRM platform and computer code language skills, in order to select the right candidate for the job.

Formal workflows, schedules and working processes need to be implemented within the marketing department and internal departments so that everyone knows what is going on, how work is to be done and when it is to be achieved by.

Within the data team, formal documentation needs to be developed to describe how tasks should be undertaken.

Staff can be trained internally, supplemented by attending any outside courses that are relevant to the role.

A new type of working culture needs to be implemented within the data team – one of supporting and developing staff so they are able to contribute effectively to the running of the CRM platform in order to help achieve organisational goals.

The CRM database manager could give the CRM database administrator data projects to be carried out to develop the skill base of the administrator and break up the monotony of completing daily/weekly routine data tasks.

If temporary members of staff are employed at any time within the data team, a system of job rotation could be employed so that they are engaged with the work they are carrying out.

A working group consisting of staff in relevant departments could be set up and meet on a regular basis to help develop the system and give them the opportunity to highlight any issues and concerns about the CRM platform that then can be addressed.

The structure of the data team may need to change and evolve to meet the growing demands placed on it.

Additional specialist staff may need to be hired, such as data analysts so that the work can be completed within the relevant deadlines.

Summary

This section has covered aspects of data team organisation, management, motivation, effective team performance and what skills and abilities are needed to manage a CRM database team.

Management is concerned with planning and organising the resources available to the data team so that it can effectively carry out the work it is responsible for in order to assist the organisation to achieve its goals.

Aspects of management the CRM database manager will be responsible for include the operation of the CRM database, human resource management and financial planning. These will include:

- training and developing staff members and the team to ensure they can meet present and future objectives;
- recruiting and selecting new team members;
- managing performance of the team and individual members;
- developing an effective team.

The attributes needed to be a successful CRM database manager are a combination of interpersonal skills such as communication, time management, organising and planning abilities, and technical knowledge.

Interpersonal abilities will enable the CRM database manager to form effective working relationships with team members, internal members of staff, external agencies and stakeholders in the CRM platform to make the system a success.

The technical knowledge and experience of the CRM database manager will help instil confidence within other team members that they are being managed by someone who has the ability to help achieve team goals and develop the CRM platform to meet future organisational objectives.

The factors that affect the efficiency of the team include:

- the size and composition of the data team in relation to the tasks it will be expected to carry out;
- the positioning of the CRM platform/data team within the organisation;
- workflows and procedures between the data team roles and how they relate to external departments and teams.

An effective CRM database manager should be able to do the following.

Advocate and be a supporter of the data team

The manager needs to be able to support the team and act as a voice for the team at executive level to ensure it has enough resources to undertake the work expected of it. The manager will be an advocate for the work that is being carried out in the data team and promote the successes and benefits of the data team in enabling the organisation to meet its goals.

Manage the team

The manager should be able to manage and support the data team in the following ways:

a) Structuring the team – each member of the team should know what their role entails and what their responsibilities are.
b) Training staff – the skills of the data team members need to be developed to meet the changing demands placed on them.
c) Motivating the team – this may become more important during times of high workloads and when lots of demands are being placed on the team or repetitive tasks need to be undertaken, such as high volumes of data processing.
d) Creating the right working environment to produce productive team members – the goal of the manager should be to create an effective working environment where team members are as productive as possible and feel that they can:

- highlight potential improvements and areas of concern within the CRM database;
- raise any issues or problems that need to be addressed in the team;
- provide feedback on projects undertaken by the data team;
- have the opportunity to implement new ideas and working practices for the data team in order to improve workflows;
- exercise their responsibility to seek help with any questions regarding their work where necessary;
- contribute to addressing problems and finding solutions to resolve any issues within the CRM database team;
- discuss new ideas, ask questions, make suggestions and provide feedback to improve ideas suggested by senior members of staff and managers;
- offer suggestions and comments that will be acted upon by managers;
- use any mistakes they make to improve working processes and guidelines and training while implementing new strategies to avoid their happening again, taking responsibility for mistakes, but learning from them so that they are not repeated;
- be free of working in a climate of fear, continuous stress and intimidation;
- take responsibility and have the confidence to undertake the work they are doing with the knowledge that support and help are available if required;
- work in an environment of continuous learning – 'What you don't know, you learn, or you ask someone how to undertake a task.'
- raise problems and issues with team members to foster a proactive approach in finding solutions to problems;
- understand the contribution and impact they make within the data team and wider organisation; this emphasises the need for the data team to have well-defined roles and structures and be positioned within the organisation correctly.

By employing some of these techniques, staff will be able to take on more responsibility and tasks within the data team. More importantly, it shows members of staff that they are continuously improving their skill sets and range of abilities and that the manager has confidence in them to complete a wide range of tasks successfully. This will also help the data team to reassign tasks and cover data tasks in unforeseen circumstances, such as when staff members are absent or when tasks need to be undertaken at short notice.

CRM database personnel work in an operational environment, and things will go wrong from time to time and unexpected events will occur that need to be dealt with. Only by working as a team will these challenges be met.

Problems and issues that occur in an operational environment need to be dealt with, and lessons learned from experience. This will also help foster team spirit in times of heavy workloads, in solving problems that are encountered and creating a learning environment that will help develop the skills and abilities of the entire data team and CRM manager. There is always something to learn in a data operations environment.

DATA IN RELATION TO MAILINGS AND REPORTS

This section will cover:

* data segmentation and management in relation to mailings and reports.

Segmentation of the data

When we talk about clearly defining data groups, this involves identifying and classifying different segments of data that are stored in the CRM platform.

How the data is divided and segmented depends entirely on the organisation.

Some methods of consumer segmentation may include geographic, demographic, geo-demographic, behavioural or transactional.

Organisational segmentation may include industry Standard Industrial Classification (SIC) codes, products and the methods included in consumer segmentation.

To segment the data, you need to ensure that you can actually store that information in the database. For example, if you want to segment organisations by industry type and no field is available on the CRM platform to record the type of industry an organisation operates in, it will be very difficult to target different industries for mailings and analyse different industry sectors in reports.

Data segmentation gaps and issues

For the data to be segmented within the database in a particular way:

- A place needs to exist for the information to be recorded within the database, such as a field within the database. For example, if you need to record industry type, there needs to be an appropriate box to record this information.
- The actual information needs to be collected and recorded within the database from data sources.

If both of these areas are not addressed, then it will be very difficult to segment the information within the database.

Issues within these areas may be caused by the following:

- How the data was to be segmented was not considered in the initial design of the database.
- The data on the CRM platform no longer meets the requirements of the organisation to achieve its goals.
- A data plan for collecting and capturing the necessary information for the organisations requirements has not been developed or implemented.
- Organisational objectives may have changed, or the business environment the company operates in may have transformed.

These factors will have created a discrepancy between the data held on the CRM database and the busines markets, consumers and other groups of people the organisation wishes to target, which will utimately mean the organisation will be unable to achieve its objectives.

These problems with data gaps and segmenting the data in the database can be resolved in the following ways:

- Plan and continually identify new data segments that will help achieve your organisational goals and objectives.
- Assess how this information is to be stored and collected/captured. This may mean liaising with other teams in the organisation to identify new segments, and assessing the current data held within the database to ensure it can meet future data requirements.
- How data is to be segmented should be a consideration when designing the initial database design, as this effects the fields/data types within the database.
- Some database platforms allow the customisation of fields and field values to add new data to existing records.
- Undertake research to fill in any missing data or add additional information that is already stored in the database so that the data can be correctly segmented.
- Ensure that the organisation has a data capture and collection plan in place.
- A gap analysis methodology should be developed and carried out on an ongoing basis to ensure that the data held by the organisation will help achieve its objectives.

This defining and segmenting should make data for mailings and reporting easier to research, locate and compile, which will ultimately help with the distribution of information throughout the organisation. It should be considered as an ongoing process to ensure the organisation's current and future data requirements are met.

Data management for reports and mailings

A system for managing the data for mailings and reports needs to be implemented within the organisation or data team.

This can largely be defined by the business processes and workflows between the data team and the rest of the organisation on how reports and mailings are produced and compiled.

MAILINGS

This section will cover:

- issues involved in undertaking and processing a mailing for a marketing campaign;
- outline of a mailing process that can be implemented within the organisation to successfully deliver communications to target segments.

Mailings or campaigns in whatever format – hard copy or electronic – will be used to promote the organisation's events and products to individuals, organisations, interest groups or relevant target segments in the database.

Mailing preference information

At the point of data capture – be it hard copy marketing literature or an electronic point of contact, such as an organisation's website – there needs to be an opportunity for potential customers to specify mailing options about:

- information on products/services/publications/events/topics they would be interested in receiving, if any; a general opt-in to receive all communication from an organisation is also an option.
- how they would like to receive this information; some people may specify more than one form of communication.

This information then needs to be recorded on the database.

Mailing data/segments

How to segment data within the database has been discussed in the 'Data in Relation to Mailings and Reports' section.

Mailing process, procedures and guidelines

Every organisation should have in place procedures and guidelines for how mailings are undertaken, including how mailing segments are agreed upon.

Marketing departments should have a schedule/timetable of mailings, campaigns and events that will occur, which will enable the data department to prepare for when data is likely to be required for them. It's important for this information to be regularly updated and the relevant team members notified of any changes so that deadlines are achieved and campaigns are delivered on schedule.

Figure 8 shows a suggested campaign mailing process.

1. Defining the mailing data brief

Factors to be considered when drawing up a data brief include:

- target groups to be included in the mailing;
- the type of mailing that is being undertaken – for example electronic or hard copy;
- the budget for the mailing and its objective.

In all cases, the target audiences need to be specifically defined so that the information can be correctly retrieved from the database.

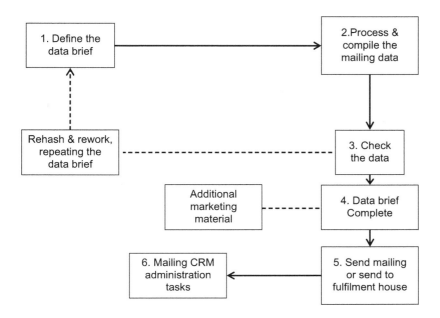

Figure 8 A proposed process for compiling campaign mailings

A data brief form, as outlined in Appendix 1, shows how each specific segment for the mailing can be defined, and includes additional information about the mailing, such as when the data is needed and the mailing numbers required.

Appendices 2 and 3 show how a small database application can be developed to keep track of mailing lists and segments. The form also serves as a platform for discussion between the marketing department and CRM administrator to correctly define the segments for each mailing. For example, the marketing department may want to target a segment that cannot be targeted as the information in the database may not exist. Action then needs to be taken to rectify this data gap for that mailing and future possible mailings.

The form is also important for auditing purposes should there be any problems or queries about the mailing in the future.

It's important to think about and define the segments for each mailing at the start of this process as much as possible.

Segments may be added or deleted for whatever reason in the future. However, this will not lead to an effective, efficient workflow if it is necessary to constantly add/remove data from mailings.

Organisations may continually use the same mailing list for regular events and mailings. Even though previous briefs are a good starting point for regular mailings, it can lead to complacency, in that data sets are not being expanded and the marketing team are relying on the same old mailing lists and contacts to achieve their goals.

The development, researching and acquisition of new data sets and sources should be an ongoing process to ensure that the data meets the future needs of the organisation.

2. Processing and compiling the mailing data

With the segments for that particular mailing defined, the data team can process and retrieve the data from the database. If the data required for the mailing is not in the database, possible courses of action include:

- researching and compiling the segment within the organisation;
- obtaining the data from a third-party provider;
- deciding not to include that segment in the mailing.

Resolving data segmentation gaps needs to be incorporated into the organisation's data capture and collection plan, if it exists.

3. Checking the mailing data

The data for mailings needs to be checked before being sent/stored/accessed by whoever has requested it.

Some of the basic checks that need to be undertaken include:

a) Mailing segments – check that the query to retrieve the data from the database matches the target segment required in the mailing and that all segments for the mailing have been retrieved from the database.

b) Duplicate data – ensure that there are no duplicates in the mailing. If your CRM database has the functionality to compile mailings within the system, when the segments for the mailing are being retrieved from the database, it may automatically take out duplicate records.

c) Formatting of the data – check the format of the data, especially when compiling postal campaigns, ensuring that addresses and postcodes are properly formatted etc. It is a common practice to format the data using a spreadsheet program – for example, sorting the data or deleting unwanted columns. After formatting the data, check it against the original data in the database to ensure that columns have not been mixed, resulting in mailings being sent to the wrong person at the wrong address.

d) Scope of the data – make sure that only the minimum amount of data that is necessary is compiled for use in the mailing. For example, for postal campaigns, you need only the address and name. You don't need to compile any further information from the database.

e) Mailing preferences and exclusions – ensure that these have been applied to suppress contacts that should not be included in the mailing. The exclusions could be inactive records, deceased records or mailing/contact types, such as 'no mail'.

f) Type of mailing – making sure the right type of mailing, for example email or postal, has been applied to the correct mailing segments.

4. Data brief completed

Once the data brief has been completed, the data can be combined with any additional marketing material.

5. Sending the mailing

The mailing can be sent out by the organisation itself, or a fulfilment house can be used to do so.

6. Mailing CRM administration tasks

After the mailing has been completed, additional CRM administration tasks may need to be undertaken, including:

- making sure a note has been made on a contact's record that they have been sent a mailing;
- logging email bounce-backs on the CRM platform and returns and responses from a hard copy mailing;
- reporting and analysis of the mailing or campaign.

Issues in regard to mailings

Rehashing, reworking, and repeating of the campaign mailing

Before the data for the mailing is considered complete and signed off, it should be checked against the original data brief.

One of the major issues to avoid is constant rehashing/reworking/repeating of the mailing due to people constantly changing the data brief. This can lead to:

- unnecessary pressure and work being imposed on the data team to complete the data brief before the mailing deadline;
- confusion among campaign teams about what groups are being targeted in a particular campaign;
- errors occurring in the generation of the mailing data – for example, exclusions and mailing preferences being applied incorrectly.

Some points that may help to avoid or help in dealing with the constant rehashing of mailings include:

a) Make sure the data brief is specific as possible – for example, the type of mailing and what segments to target.

    If there are any queries about the data brief, make sure these are resolved before the data is compiled. This could entail contacting the people running the campaign to fully understand their data requirements.

    Ensure that there is sufficient time for staff to make any changes and that they have fully thought through who needs to be contacted in a particular mailing before starting to compile it.

b) Set specific deadlines when the last changes can be made.

    Make sure final decisions for the data brief for the campaign are clearly communicated to the campaign team so you have time to compile the data.

    Plan, schedule and agree timelines for the compiling of the mailings.

    Explain to the campaign team that it does sometimes take more time than might be anticipated to compile the data.

Mailing schedule planner

A mailing schedule planner needs to be developed so that departments involved in mailings can plan ahead to ensure that deadlines are achieved.

Accessing and storing the mailing data

Ideally, the data should be stored centrally.

    Some database platforms have built-in functionality to compile campaign/ mailing lists. As long as users have the correct access rights, they can view the campaign/mailings within the CRM platform.

    If this is not possible, the data can be stored centrally on the organisation's network as long as the necessary security measures are in place – for example, file and folder access restrictions on users are set correctly.

    Here are some basic guidelines for storing mailing queries and reports wherever they are stored:

- Organise reports and data extracts for mailings into relevant group folders.
- Ensure that the naming system for reports and mailings is consistent throughout the organisation.
- Users should only have access to the mailing data and reports they are working on.
- Files should not be stored on a local desktop.

Sending the data to third-party organisations

If data needs to be sent to a third-party mailing house, then security needs to be assessed and methods implemented accordingly. This may include encrypting files and using a secure network so that a data breach does not occur.

It is essential to check that third-party organisations are complying with any relevant data legislation when they are managing or processing your organisation's data on your behalf.

Using third-party applications in mailings

An organisation may use third-party applications such as email marketing applications. This may cause data inconsistency, for example due to bounce-backs of emails not being recorded on the CRM platform.

If the organisation has chosen to use a third-party application, make sure that it is synchronised or integrated with the CRM platform so that the record it contains is updated accordingly. This will help to keep the data clean and maintain data quality while providing the marketing team with a complete record of that campaign/contact. It will also assist in the analysis and reporting of the mailing.

Using the CRM platform in mailings

The CRM platform can be used to send the necessary mailing material to the segments within the data brief, depending on the functionality of the CRM platform. For example:

- Email campaigns can be sent using the CRM email functionality.
- Mailing letters can be produced within the CRM platform, if it has this functionality.

Auditing of the mailing data and process

Reporting will need to be undertaken on the various mailings sent out by the organisation to provide feedback and analysis on the success of campaigns and to see whether they achieved their overall objectives.

In addition to the reporting and the analysis of the actual mailing, an audit could be undertaken of the mailing process itself to identify and rectify errors and issues so that the management of future mailings will be more effective and efficient.

Case study

Data XYZ PLC undertakes mailings for both hard copy and email marketing campaigns.

The organisation has encountered various problems when undertaking mailing campaigns, from compiling the data right through to recording the outcomes from a particular campaign.

Sales staff are engaging in information scraping from website and hard copy sales literature, compiling lists and using a desktop application to send emails to potential clients.

Even when the mailing has been co-ordinated by the marketing team, the same mailing has sometimes been sent out twice.

The data has been found to have duplicate information in the mailing lists, causing multiple emails and hard copies to be sent to the same person.

No thought has gone into the targeting or what segments are to be used for a mailing. Marketing segments the organisation would like to target are not listed or available for use within the CRM platform.

The marketing team thought it would be a good idea to contact the entire list of contacts on the database who gave an email address to promote their products.

During a hard copy mailing, marketing material was sent to deceased and inactive contacts.

No exclusions or mailing preferences have been recorded against a contacts record.

The organisation uses a third-party email platform that is not connected or synchronised with the main CRM platform, so bounce-backs have not been recorded on the CRM database.

No schedule of mailings exists in the marketing department, causing mailings to be generated at the last minute or being sent late.

There are no formal workflow processes in the department for producing and generating a mailing – for example, there are no formal data briefs or procedures for dealing with returns and email bounce-backs. This is causing additional work to be generated, as mailings are constantly rehashed and reworked to send the right content to the right recipients.

Possible improvements in this case study scenario

The mailing process needs to be formalised within the marketing department.

Data tasks relating to the mailing should be undertaken by the data team. However, the management and co-ordination of the entire mailing process should be the responsibility of the marketing team.

Workflows, procedures, guidelines and schedules needs to be developed so that everyone knows what is expected of them and when it is supposed to happen.

Schedules for mailings and deadlines for work need to be outlined and communicated to the entire department.

A mailing planner should also be developed by the marketing department and made available to the data team so that the data work involved in the production of a mailing can be organised appropriately.

Target segments that are unavailable for the mailing could be collected or acquired from a third-party source. The organisation needs to update and plan ahead its data capture strategy to ensure that information required for future mailings is available.

Sales staff engaging in the practice of information scraping from electronic sources and hard copy formats and sending unsolicited marketing material needs to be addressed and stopped. These practices may have legal implications, reflect badly on the organisation, and will tarnish, if not seriously damage, the organisation's brand.

Mailing preferences and exclusions need to recorded and updated on the contacts record and abided by.

If people request not to receive emails, then the organisation should not send them emails.

Checks should be carried out to ensure that any exclusions have been applied to the mailing. These may include records that are recorded as deceased or inactive and any mailing preference opt-outs. In the case of hard copy mailing, contacts with no valid address need to be excluded from mailing runs.

A formal data brief needs to written for every mailing, outlining:

- the segments that are to be targeted in the campaign;
- the type of mailing – email or hard copy;
- the timeline, deadlines and schedule for the mailing.

This will help reduce the rehashing of the mailing and avoiding additional work for the data team.

Before the mailing is sent out, the data team should check for duplicates in the mailing list.

For postal campaigns, the format of the data should be checked – for example, that the initial letters of names are capitalised and postcodes are in upper case.

After the data has been correctly formatted, it might be an idea for someone to check the data for any errors.

The mailing data should be checked against the source data in the CRM database to make sure that names and addresses/email addresses are correct and have not been reformatted incorrectly.

When the data has been collected, compiled, cleaned and sent, the mailing needs to be recorded on the contacts record so that it is not sent out twice.

Procedures for dealing with email bounce-backs and mailing returns need to be implemented.

If a third-party email application is to be used instead of the organisation's CRM platform email system, they need to be synchronised so that bounce-backs are recorded.

SLAs to clean the returned data need to be developed so that the data is as up-to-date as possible for the next mailing to be compiled. Contact records need to be updated accordingly: deceased, gone away, change of address/contact details etc.

This will also help improve the overall quality of the data in the CRM database.

Seeding the data with contact details of an individual within the organisation is one way to check the mailing has been sent.

Summary

Mailings are used to inform contacts about an organisation's services and products. They are also used to enhance the relationship between the organisation and the customer.

This relationship can be damaged if a contact's mailings preferences are not respected and processed correctly.

This puts an emphasis on the quality of the information in the database, especially in relation to setting up a contact's mailing preferences correctly and updating this information when appropriate and ensuring that contacts have the correct mailing and email addresses attributed to them within the database.

A process needs to be implemented for the production of mailing campaigns, which could include:

- defining the data brief;
- compiling the data;
- checking the data brief and making any changes if necessary;
- ensuring that the completed data is combined with additional marketing material;
- ensuring that the mailing is sent to the relevant contacts;
- additional CRM data tasks to compile a complete record of the communications sent to a contact.

The stages for data in marketing campaigns can be summed up in the Six Cs:

- Collect
- Combine
- Clean
- Check
- Communicate
- Critique.

The data team and marketing department need to schedule when data is required for various campaigns. This schedule should be updated and reviewed on an ongoing basis so that work can be planned ahead and data deadlines met.

The information needs to be as clean as possible before a mailing is sent out, and a process for dealing with any email bounce-backs or hard copy mailing returns needs to be implemented. This will help the organisation form a relationship with its customers in order to meet its objectives. It will also help in financial terms by:

- reducing costs by not spending money on unnecessary postage and targeting customers more effectively;
- avoiding losing customers and potential customers by sending unnecessary and unwanted mailings;
- the organisation paying out penalty fines for being in breach of any data legislation.

REPORTING AND ANALYSIS

This section will cover:

- issues involved in undertaking reporting and analysis within the organisation;
- outlining a reporting process that can be implemented within the organisation;
- the types of analysis that can be undertaken on the data within the CRM database;
- the presentation and visualisation of the data.

If the data within the CRM platform has achieved organisational data quality standards, it can be analysed, interpreted and reported on so that it can:

- be used by executive stakeholders to make informed decisions about the organisation;
- help to ensure that goals and objectives are being achieved;
- identify possible new business opportunities for the organisation.

Reporting guidelines and procedures

Reporting guidelines and procedures should be implemented to improve efficiency and workflows within the organisation. The following procedures and guidelines need to be considered.

Formatting of reports

Organisations will have their own guidelines on how internal reports are to be formatted. These could include:

- the styling of the report;
- what data needs to be included;
- naming conventions;
- who needs the report;
- types of reports needed;
- frequency of reports;
- types of graphs/visual data to be used;
- format.

The formatting of the report may be done by the CRM application, or it may need to be exported to a third-party application like a spreadsheet or a reporting software platform may be used.

The reporting process

As with mailings, a reporting process needs to be implemented within the organisation.

The process for delivering a mailing can be adapted and used as a template to define the reporting process:

1 Defining the report – some of the factors that apply to the reporting brief have been outlined above in the discussion of formatting.
2 Compiling the report – the necessary data is retrieved from the database. The data is then compiled into the required format for presentation purposes.
3 Checking the report – the report is checked against the original reporting brief.
4 Sending the report – the report is distributed to the person or group of people that requested it.

Issues of reporting and analysis

Rehashing and reworking of reports

As with mailings, there is a danger that you will get into an endless cycle of rehashing, repeating and reworking the report.

Reporting schedule and requests

Reports may be needed at various times of the month, year or week. A reporting schedule needs to be implemented so that everyone is aware what reports are needed, when they are required and who within the organisation needs them.

Most reports are required at a specific time, but a report request form could be set up for any ad hoc reports that may be needed (similar to the data mailing form in Appendix 1).

Generation and management of reports

Who is responsible for generating and compiling reports and how the reporting is to be undertaken needs to be considered.

If reports are to be generated centrally by the data team, queries for standard reports can be developed to be reused, to avoid duplication of work.

However, some organisations have a team or department responsible for generating and formatting reports.

How reports are generated may depend on the functionality of the CRM platform or how the reporting tasks have been organised within the data team. For example, some CRM platforms allow for reports to be scheduled, formatted and run automatically. This feature can be used by the data team to set up a query to retrieve the relevant data, schedule and format the report. Based on the defined schedule, the report is updated and those who require it will be automatically informed by email when it is ready to be viewed.

Alternatively, the data team can run the reporting queries manually, format the data according to the organisational reporting style, and send the report to the report requester manually.

Another option might be third-party reporting software that would need to be integrated into the CRM platform and used by the data team.

Storing reports

How the procedure for reports is implemented within the organisation will affect how reports are stored and accessed.

Security considerations for staff in regard to reporting include:

- Who is able to compile reports?
- Who should have access to the completed reports?

If the CRM platform has the functionality, then reports can be stored within it. An alternative solution is to use the organisation's own network as long as the necessary security measures have been considered, such as user access to the folder containing the reports.

Analysis of information

How the organisation analyses its data needs to be considered.

Organisations can employ or hire data analysts with a statistical/mathematical background who have worked within a data environment and are familiar with analysing data.

Third-party organisations can provide reporting and analytical services for specific campaigns/events or organisational data sets.

By analysing the data held on the CRM platform, the organisation may:

- better understand its customers' behaviour and business environment;
- identify new trends;
- identify new target markets and opportunities;
- improving decision-making in order to meet organisational objectives;
- tailor its products and services to its customers;
- discover financial benefits, such saving and making money through improved efficiencies and the ability to meet consumers' needs.

Quality of reporting

It should be noted that the analysis and reports produced will only be as good as the information that is held within the CRM database.

Reporting and analysis software

There are various options available for an organisation to undertake reporting and analysis.

Reporting

a) CRM reporting module – most, if not all, CRM solutions come with their own reporting module.
b) Combining software applications – some organisations query the data and export it to a desktop application such as a spreadsheet to be correctly formatted into the organisation's reporting style.
c) Reporting software – third-party reporting applications can be employed to generate reports which are integrated into the CRM platform if an organisation needs to report and analyse the CRM platform data set.

Analytics

The types of tools used to analysis the data can also vary. This will largely depend on the resources the organisation has available.

The types of analytical tools available include one or a combination of the following:

a) Desktop applications – spreadsheet and database applications are used to interrogate the data.
b) Specialist analytical software – this can be employed to analyse the data.
c) CRM analytical module/third-party analytical software – if the CRM platform has an analytical module, this could be used, or third-party analytics software could be integrated into the CRM platform.
d) Data warehouse – a data warehouse can be developed by the organisation to analyse the data held on a CRM platform.
e) Artificial intelligence (AI) –AI is being developed by CRM platform vendors and technology organisations to improve the analysis, interpretation and understanding of data sets, including the data held on a CRM platform.

Types of analysis

There are various types of analysis that can be undertaken on the data. 'Six Types of Analysis Every Data Scientist Should Know' (Leek, 2013)[38] identifies six of them:

1 Descriptive – this involves identifying characteristics of different data sets/ groups within the data. An example would be different market segments in a customer database.

---

38 Leek, J. (Professor of Biostatistics and Oncology at John Hopkins Bloomberg School of Public Health) (2013), 'Six Types of Analysis Every Data Scientist Should Know', http://datascientistinsights. com/2013/01/29/six-types-of-analyses-every-data-scientist-should-know/.

2   Exploratory – this method of analysis is used to find previously unknown rela-tionships between different variables – for example, is there a link between gender, age and types of holiday taken?
3   Inferential – this method is used to test theories about the world in general – for example, does age have anything to do with the level of car accidents that occur?
4   Predictive – in this method, historical and present data is used to predict future events. An example would be analysing buyer behaviour to target cus-tomers with future products and sales offers.
5   Causal – this involves analysing the relationships between different variables when one variable is altered or changed, for example, age or gender.
6   Mechanistic – this method tries to explain how changes in one variable, such as age, lead to changes in other variables.

Data visualisation and infographics

When the analysis has been completed, its results need to presented so that the feedback and findings can be acted upon within the business environment. At this stage, how the data is presented becomes an important consideration.

Data visualisation and infographics are concerned with how data is presented using images, text and graphics.

In relation to CRM platforms, the most common types of data visualisation probably involve producing reports and dashboards.

Data visualisation is becoming more and more important, with a variety of software and products becoming available to show the outcomes of data analysis. When developing content to display data analysis results, some important factors need to be taken into consideration:

a)   Keep the audience in mind – are they business people or more scientific, analytical individuals? The type of audience will affect the type of visuals used.
b)   Data platform – take into consideration the platform the information will be viewed on. How a graphic/text looks on a mobile phone and how it appears on presentation software may be completely different.
c)   Content – bear in mind that symbols, colours, text and images may have dif-ferent meanings for different cultures and audiences.

Case study

Data XYZ PLC is missing reporting deadlines, and no analysis is undertaken on the data held in the CRM database.

Possible improvements in this case study scenario

To improve the efficiency of the reporting within the CRM team, reporting sched-ules should be drawn to outline:

- who the report is for;
- when it is due;
- the format in which the report will be presented.

The CRM team could look into the possibility of automating some reporting functions, such as storing and reusing queries relating to reports to reduce the lag time in producing, formatting distributing them to the recipients.

If the organisation's CRM platform has reporting functionality that can schedule reports to be run automatically, then this could be used by the data team to meet reporting deadlines.

Procedures should be put into place and communicated throughout the organisation to set out how to make requests for new reports and data analysis.

Further investigation into third-party reporting and analysis software could be undertaken to ensure the organisation's present and future reporting and analytical demands are met.

The possibility of contracting or recruiting a data analyst to better understand and interrogate the data held on the database should be considered.

Summary

An audit of an organisation's reporting and analysis processes needs to be undertaken, including existing reporting and analytical procedures and the type of software used for these purposes.

Procedures and guidelines need to be implemented for reporting to ensure that the reporting workflows are able to meet organisational needs and deadlines.

How reports are developed, executed, formatted and analysed and who is responsible for undertaking these tasks needs to be organised within the business or specific data team.

What type of data analysis is undertaken on the CRM data will depend largely on what the organisation wants to find out in relation to its data set.

The reporting and analysis of the data will be closely linked to the overall goals of the organisation. This could include discovering new market segments or even predicting future buying habits of consumers.

After the analysis has been completed, the findings need to communicated in a way that the relevant audience understands, but also provide a platform for the relevant individuals to act upon that information and, if necessary, help in the decision-making process.

The important point to remember is that the analysis and reports produced will only be as good as the information held in the CRM database.

DATA MIGRATIONS

This section will cover:

- the process of undertaking a data migration.

Data migration is the moving of data from one or more data sources to another storage medium, such as a CRM platform. Each data migration will be unique, depending on the data and the CRM platform involved.

However, common stages in any data migration project are necessary to ensure its success. This section will look at the key tasks that need to be undertaken in all data migration projects.

Issues in regard to data migrations

Schedule and plan the data migration

It's important to schedule and plan the data migration in order to ensure that:

- any disruptions the data migration project may cause are minimised;
- no data is lost or corrupted;
- deadlines and timelines are achieved and that the project remains on track;
- the necessary financial, technical, and human resources are available to make the project a success.

This could be the responsibility of an individual, or a working group of various stakeholders within the organisation could be set up to ensure the project is completed within the specified deadlines.

Communication

Communication will also be important during the data migration project. This may entail:

- notifying users, where appropriate, of any database downtime while the data migration is under way;
- updating the rest of the organisation about how the project is proceeding and promoting the work that is being undertaken;
- liaising with data migration project stakeholders and team members to ensure the success of the project.

The data migration project process

The following aspects of the data migration process will be looked at in more detail:

1   project and data audit;
2   developing data transformation guidelines;
3   validating/cleaning and formatting the data before migration;
4   developing software and tools to aid the migration;
5   testing the data before migration;
6   preparing and undertaking the data migration;
7   cleaning and checking the data after migration.

1. Project and data audit

The project audit will consist of looking at the technical, financial and human resources needed to make the data migration project a success. The following information about the data to be migrated also needs to be audited:

a) Columns and tables – this will include looking at data values, data types, data sizes, indexes and formats.
b) Table structures and relationships – the relationships between different tables will need to be identified. This is important as it will affect the order in which the data is migrated/imported into the database. For example, before contact data can be migrated, the account information needs to be imported, otherwise it will not be possible to link the contacts to the right organisations. Most database platforms may have a built-in facility to produce documentation and reports on the database schema, table, column information and table relationships that form the basis of the CRM database.
c) The amount of data to be migrated – this will affect how long the migration takes and the choice of technical tools and processes to be used. The number of rows in each table to be migrated to the new database should be established. This can provide a check at the end of the migration process to ensure the data import has been successful.
d) Data file types – the file format of the data to be migrated will need to be taken into consideration. This may affect:

- what tools are used;
- how the data is validated;
- what format the data will be consolidated into before migration.

2. Developing data transformation guidelines

This stage of the process can also be called column mapping. Columns in the old database need to be mapped to the field columns in the new database.

If fields in the new database are not matched with the fields in the old database, the data cannot be transferred.

Some CRM platforms allow for some customisation of the database. New fields can be created in the new database to accommodate the information that needs to be migrated – for example, unique IDs from the old database.

3. Validating/cleaning and formatting the data before migration

When the data transformation (column mapping) stage has been completed, data cleaning and formatting can begin, to ensure that the data to be imported adheres to the data rules of the new database.

Aspects of the data that will need to be validated and cleaned are:

a) Null values – ensure that any null values in the old database are to be null values in the new database and that these values are valid in the new database.

b) Mandatory fields – ensure that if mandatory fields are required in the new database, data exists in these fields in the old database or that the information is provided and updated before migrating the data.

c) Value ranges – data to be migrated must be within any value ranges that are constrained in the mapped column in the new database.

d) Data values – ensure that if the columns require only certain values, those are the values provided in the data migration. If values from the data to be migrated need to be accommodated in the new database, update them in the new database so that it matches the corresponding field in the old database, to avoid errors – for example, if you have a countries pick list field that has a value of USA in the old database the value needs to be USA in the new database.

e) Data formats – ensure that data is in the correct format for the mapped column. For example, should dates be in American format or UK format, and are they in a long or short format?

f) Data types – ensuring that the data to be migrated to the mapped column is of the same data type. For example, if a mapped column is numeric, ensure that the data is not in a date format.

g) Duplicate values – these need to be tested on:

- Column or Field level: If data is being migrated to a column where it is a primary key or has to be a unique value, duplicate values need to be tested for in the data before the migration takes place or an error will occur when the data is imported in the CRM platform.
- Data Set: Testing for actual duplicate records within the data set. e.g. contacts that are the same will need to be tested for in the data to be migrated. These records can then be consolidated and merged as appropriate.

Testing for duplicates will be increasingly important if you have to merge and combine multiple data sets before undertaking the data migration.

Software tools for data cleaning

BESPOKE SOFTWARE

Bespoke software can be developed or purchased to validate, clean and format the data to be migrated. Depending on the software solution selected, data errors found can then either be manually changed, automatically changed by the software, or computer code can be written to modify the data to ensure it matches the business rules of the mapped column the data is to be stored in.

DATABASE PLATFORM TECHNOLOGY

Some enterprise databases have data quality and profiling tools that can also help in cleaning data before migrating it into the database.

OPEN SOURCE SOFTWARE

Using open source software could also be another option to transform the data into the proper format before importing the data into the new database.

DESKTOP APPLICATIONS

Desktop applications like spreadsheets and database programs could also be used to clean the data before migrating it.

4. Developing software and tools to aid the migration

A wide array of tools and technology could be used in the data migration process.

DATABASE PLATFORM TECHNOLOGY

Enterprise-level database platforms include ETL (extract, transform and load) and data management tools that can be used in the migration of data between systems. Their functions may include:

- mapping different columns between the old and new databases and any other data file formats that need to be imported;
- data formatting and transformation;
- data matching;
- data cleaning.

USING THE IMPORT TOOLS OF THE CRM DATABASE

CRM platforms have import tools and wizards that allow data to be imported into a new database. This usually requires the setting up of import templates in a data format like comma-separated values (CSV).

Column headings in the template match the fields in the database the data will be imported into.

The database platform will validate the data to be imported. If any errors occur during the importing process, the data will not be imported. The data errors will need to be corrected before the information can be successfully imported.

Import tools usually need the data to be in a particular file format, which can be an issue when the data to be migrated is stored in a file format that is not compatible with the new database's import tools.

PURCHASING SOFTWARE AND MIGRATION TECHNOLOGY

Organisations can purchase third-party software import tools that are compatible with the file format the data needs to be in to allow importation into the new database. The software selected to undertake the import may include additional functionality, such as data cleaning and formatting.

Software to undertake a data migration may also be cloud-based, which may be more financially attractive to some organisations.

DEVELOPING BESPOKE TECHNOLOGY

The organisation can also develop its own software applications and technology that will aid the importation of the data into the new database.

5. *Testing the data before migration*

Before undertaking the final data migration, the data migration process needs to be tested, to check and verify the following areas:

- data validation and cleaning;
- column mapping;
- import templates;
- the order of importing files or order of data transfer – due to the table relationships within the database data may need to be added in a specific sequence so that any dependent changes are reflected in the new database;
- software and migration tools;
- software code;
- training of staff if data needs to be imported using the CRM platform's import tools.

The procedures and time involved in testing before the live data migration will vary depending on the complexity of the database and the data.

The objectives of testing are to ensure that:

- the data is migrated within the relevant timeframe;
- the data is correctly formatted and adheres to the rules of the new database;
- the data is correctly referenced;
- any errors are resolved before the live data migration is undertaken.

These are the common stages in any testing process:

a) Set up a test database – its structure should reflect that of the database the data is to be migrated to.
b) Import sample files into the test database – test data transfers and import sample files/data into the test database so that the results can be reviewed.
c) Analyse results of the test imports – after samples of data have been imported into the test database, the results of the migration need to be analysed and reviewed.

Analysis of the data migration can be undertaken by:

- setting up various reports to analyse the data imported;
- reviewing error messages and import exception files;
- setting up seed records to review data at various stages of the import so that if errors occur, you know at what stage of the import something went wrong.
- take samples of data and compare them to the original data set; this may include checking contact, organisational and financial information and ensuring that these aspects of the data are correctly referenced.
- if data has been migrated using individual data feed files, check that each file has been migrated successfully by comparing the outcome with the original data set.

d) Review results of the test data migration – if errors occur in the test imports, go back and review the data migration procedure until all the errors have been highlighted and resolved. Make any changes to the data or import procedure as appropriate before the live data migration can be undertaken.

6. Preparing and undertaking the data migration

When the data migration process has been tested and any errors and problems have been resolved, the live data migration can be carried out.

Backing up the data before import

Ensure that a backup of the target database is taken before the data migration is started. These backups should be updated regularly if a lot of files need to be imported. If errors or problems occur, the database can then be rolled back to its state before they happened. The problems can then be resolved and the import process continued.

Staging and undertaking the data migration

Data can be imported in stages, and not in one go. Any problems can then be resolved as the data is imported into the new database.

This is especially important if data needs to be imported in a particular order, as any errors occurring in the early stages of the migration can have a knock-on effect on data imported later.

If data needs to be imported in a particular order, ensure that any problems or errors are resolved before the next batch of data is imported into the database.

Scheduling the data migration

Users should be told when the migration is to be undertaken and whether it is likely to affect CRM database performance. Alternatively, the data migration could be scheduled to take place out of working hours or at off-peak usage times.

Time should also be allocated to resolve any issues during the migration and to review and assess that the data migration has been completed successfully.

7. Cleaning and checking the data after migration

After the data has been imported into the live database, the data migration needs to be reviewed and audited. Additional checks and cleaning of the data that could be implemented include:

- asking staff to review records and data they are familiar with;
- adjusting and correcting any data anomalies that have occurred during the migration so that the imported data matches the original data set;
- comparing the trial data migration results with the live data migration results and original data set.

Additional related data migration tasks

In addition to the data migration itself, other tasks have to be scheduled and undertaken, possibly running in parallel with the migration.

Documentation and procedures

Documentation and procedures should be updated to reflect the new features and functions of the new CRM database.

Previous procedures from the old CRM platform can be used as a starting point to generate new guidelines for how the new CRM platform will be operated and managed within the organisation.

New workflows and processes between teams and departments need to be developed so that the information flow into and out of the CRM database is as efficient as possible.

Training staff

Staff need to be trained in the new CRM platform. Training needs to be organised around aspects of the new database that relate to their job function and the tasks they will be undertaking.

If necessary, new training material, resources and courses will need to be developed to support the ongoing needs of the staff operating the new CRM platform.

Procedures need to be tested and refined. Staff need the opportunity to put their training into practice before working with the live database. Giving staff access to a training database can help to reinforce training and refine procedures.

Case study

In a drive to improve data quality, Data XYZ PLC has identified data silos within its marketing department.

This data needs to be migrated to the CRM platform. Analysis shows that:

- The data is held in various formats.
- The data in the various files comprises contact information.
- In total, there about 10,000 records.

Possible improvements in this case study scenario

To start the process of migrating the data to the database, a basic audit could be undertaken.

The migration audit could identify that:

1   the data is in different file formats – this means it needs to be compiled into one format before importing it into the database;
2   the data consists of contact details – as this is the only data to be imported into the CRM platform, it can be imported in one file;
3   the amount of data is 10,000 records –this determines how the organisation will import the data into the CRM database.

In this case, due to the amount of data and the data being in different file formats, an import tool could be used to check for duplicates by comparing the data within the CRM database and the data to be imported.

Using the field headings within the database, a spreadsheet import template could be developed.

The data from the various data sources could be combined and reformatted in the import template so that the correct data is placed under the correct headings in the spreadsheet to be imported into the database.

The data could be reformatted using spreadsheet functions to format the data – capitalisation of forenames etc.

After this initial reformatting of the data, the data could be processed using various data quality tools and services to ensure it has been correctly formatted before importing the data file into the CRM platform.

Examples of reformatting the data could include ensuring that postcodes are formatted correctly and checking that the number of digits in phone numbers is correct. The file could then be uploaded into the import tool, which would automatically match the import template headings to the fields in the database.

The importing of the contacts into the CRM platform could now be undertaken. Using the import tool, if the contacts in the import file matched the records already in the CRM system, they would be updated, or if they did not exist, they would be added as new contacts.

The data could then be checked against the original source files.

Staff could be asked to check and provide feedback on the data that has been migrated into the CRM platform to ensure that it has been imported successfully.

Summary

Data migrations can be complex tasks, and potentially takes months to plan and execute.

This puts an emphasis on strong project management skills and defining clear project milestones, goals and objectives.

In addition to a clear methodology being defined and outlined for transferring data to the new system, appropriate resources and time need to be allocated so that the data migration can be a success.

A data migration process will include the following stages:

- analysis;
- mapping;
- data cleaning and transformation;
- testing;
- importing;
- checking.

SECURITY

This section will cover:

- a framework to deal with data breaches of the CRM platform;
- a framework to undertake a risk assessment of possible threats to the CRM data;
- an outline of the types of threats to an organisation's CRM data.

As data is important asset to an organisation, it needs to be protected like any other resource.

The type of threats the CRM database is exposed to and who is responsible for securing the information can depend on:

- whether the CRM database is stored locally or a third party hosts it;
- whether the CRM database has been integrated into the company website;
- security policies implemented within the organisation;
- guidelines and procedures for the disposal and use of data within the organisation.

Defining risk

According to the FAIR methodology (The Open Group, 2010, p.41),[39] risk can be defined as: 'The probable frequency and probable magnitude of future loss'.

Other methodologies have their own definition, of how risk is defined.

However, the PCI Security Standards Council (November 2012, p.3)[40] outlines that risk includes different elements that must be understood by the organisation. These include:

- the different types of threat;
- the probability of those threats occurring;
- the organisational assets that need to be protected;
- how vulnerable the organisation is to different types of threats;
- the impact a threat occurring will have on the organisation;
- how the organisation can reduce the impact or likelihood of threats being realised.

Risk management methodology

A risk management methodology needs to be implemented within the organisation. As part of this process, a risk assessment should be undertaken to identify potential threats to the CRM database.

By identifying potential threats, technical solutions and policies can be implemented to deal with them.

Types of frameworks/methodologies for conducting a risk assessment

A number of bodies have developed risk assessment frameworks and methodologies that can be used to analyse the threats to a CRM database or an entire organisation, as outlined by the PCI Security Standards Council (November 2012, p.7).[41] These bodies include:

- the National Institute of Standards and Technology (NIST);
- the International Organization of Standardization (ISO).

A number of frameworks can also be used to assess risks and threats, such as:

- Operationally Critical Threat, Asset, and Vulnerability Evaluation (OCTAVE);
- Factor Analysis of Information Risk (FAIR);
- Australian/New Zealand Standard AS/NZS 4360.

39 The Open Group (2010), *Technical Guide FAIR – ISO/IEC27005 Cookbook*, Reading, UK: The Open Group.
40 PCI Security Standards Council (November 2012), *Information Supplement: PCI DSS Risk Assessment Guidelines Version 1.0*, Wakefield, UK: PCI Security Standards Council.
41 PCI Security Standards Council (November 2012), *Information Supplement: PCI DSS Risk Assessment Guidelines Version 1.0*, Wakefield, UK: PCI Security Standards Council.

The risk management process described in this text is outlined by Baxter (2010, pp.7–8).[42] However, the different methodologies broadly follow the same process when managing risk.

The steps involved in a risk management process cover two areas:

Risk assessment – this stage deals with:

1   risk identification;
2   risk analysis;
3   risk prioritisation.

Risk control – this stage deals with:

4   risk management planning;
5   risk mitigation/resolution;
6   monitor and review.

Risk assessment

1. Risk identification

When trying to understand the risks an organisation faces, we need to look at the following dimensions: assets, vulnerabilities, impacts and threats, as outlined by The Open Group (2010)[43] and PCI Security Standards Council (November 2012).[44]

Assets

The Open Group (2010, p.39)[45] states that an asset can be defined as: 'Any data, device, or other component of the environment that supports information-related activities, which can be illicitly accessed, used, disclosed, altered, destroyed, and/or stolen, resulting in loss'. An example would be the data that is held within the CRM platform.

Vulnerabilities

Vulnerability can be defined as stated by The Open Group (2010, p.43):[46] 'The probability that an asset will be unable to resist actions of a threat agent'.

This involves assessing how well an asset can deal with a particular risk.

42 Baxter, K. (2010), *Risk Management*, London: Pearson Education Limited.
43 The Open Group (2010), *Technical Guide FAIR – ISO/IEC27005 Cookbook*, Reading, UK: The Open Group.
44 PCI Security Standards Council (November 2012), *Information Supplement: PCI DSS Risk Assessment Guidelines Version 1.0*, Wakefield, UK: PCI Security Standards Council.
45 The Open Group (2010), *Technical Guide FAIR – ISO/IEC27005 Cookbook*, Reading, UK: The Open Group.
46 The Open Group (2010), *Technical Guide FAIR – ISO/IEC27005 Cookbook*, Reading, UK: The Open Group.

Vulnerabilities are weaknesses that can be exploited by technology, people and processes that may cause damage to the functioning of the organisation.

Vulnerabilities may include poorly designed and written software, but also poorly designed business processes.

Impacts

Impact can be defined as the effect on an organisation should a threat be realised. This can manifest in several ways, for instance:

- in financial terms, such as a drop in share price, financial loss or loss of equipment;
- the organisation not being able to conduct 'business as usual';
- other intangible effects, such as loss of consumer confidence in the organisation or damage to its brand.

Threats

A threat can be defined as stated by The Open Group (2010, p.42):[47] 'Anything that is capable of acting in a manner resulting in harm to an asset and/or organisation'.

Threats can be either technological, the result of poorly designed processes or be posed by people.

Some of the risks and threats to an organisation and the CRM database are outlined below.

INTERNAL THREATS

Recruitment of staff   The human resources department should have policies in place to ensure it recruits the correct staff – for example, background and criminal record checks and employer references. This to prevent staff selling data to third parties or undertaking malicious acts by deleting/destroying data.

Database security considerations   The CRM database administrator will primarily be concerned with ensuring that users have the right permissions to control who can access what data and to undertake the necessary data manipulation tasks based on their role within the organisation – for example, editing/deleting data – in addition to the type of data they can manipulate, such as contact or account data.

This may also include whether a member of staff can view reports, run queries and export data.

---

47 The Open Group (2010), *Technical Guide FAIR – ISO/IEC27005 Cookbook*, Reading, UK: The Open Group.

Information technology security   Other ways of securing data and an organisa-tion's computer network resources need to be considered. These may include:

- being aware of new security threats to the organisation's network and keeping employees informed of the security risks;
- keeping anti-virus and business application software updated;
- making sure the firewall is correctly installed and configured;
- reviewing and promoting security policies throughout the organisation;
- reviewing and documenting staff access to folders and files on the network;
- liaising with the IT department to ensure that security policies are being adhered to;
- explaining internet and IT policies when inducting new staff members;
- ensuring that any software developed internally is rigorously tested for security flaws and implementing coding guidelines for it;
- train staff in how data is to be managed within the organisation.

Storage of data   The storage of data can be a problem when:

- staff within the organisation can export data from the database and store the data in various formats on their desktops;
- staff would like to store and use data on USB sticks or laptops;
- data is stored in third-party data centres.

The following solutions can be implemented:

- Encrypt any data taken outside the organisation and password-protect files and folders on USB sticks and laptops. Set up procedures to ensure this is done, such as checking and signing a document that confirms these precau-tions have been taken.
- All data is sensitive and important, but in particular review how data such as financial and personal information is stored.
- Remote users within the organisation should use a secure network.
- If data is stored on third-party data servers, ensure that a secure network con-nection is used.
- Ensure that staff have the correct permissions and that they can't export data from the database if they don't need to do so as part of their day-to-day work.

Internally developed software   Software that is developed internally may be a security risk if it is poorly developed or poorly written and allows somebody to gain unauthorised access to the organisation's data.

EXTERNAL THREATS

The following is not a definitive list of threats to an organisation's data, but shows the wide, ever-changing and varied techniques that can be used to breach security.

Malicious programs

a) Viruses – this is malicious computer code that infects a computer or computer network to capture or corrupt data.
b) Malware – this is malicious software that is installed on a computer or network to gain access and alter, obtain or destroy information.
c) Key logging software – when this infects a computer, it records the victim's keystrokes and sends this information back to the perpetrator. The aim of this type of attack is to obtain sensitive information such as passwords and usernames so that the perpetrator can then gain access to further sensitive information.
d) Trojans – these are programs that are downloaded by users who think they are installing a legitimate piece of software. However, the software will allow the perpetrator to gain unauthorised access to information within the organisation.
e) Worms – this is malicious code that self-replicates across a network to infect computers and corrupt information within the organisation.

Hardware and software attacks   Intruders can try to gain access to an organisation's systems by exploiting any vulnerabilities in its hardware and software.

Internet/website threats   As the Web has developed, CRM systems have developed from standalone systems to platforms that are becoming increasingly integrated with an organisation's website and online strategy for the collection of information, online ecommerce/transactions/payments and promotion.

The internet also poses a threat of the CRM database being compromised by people wishing to steal information from an organisation's database.

This section outlines some potential methods criminals or malicious individuals can employ to gain access to a database:

a) Email attacks – attackers can send false emails to organisations enticing unsuspecting staff members to inadvertently download malicious software to gain access to the database or send a URL to a website to gain personal details.
b) Password attacks – this is when an attacker tries to gain access to the database by cracking passwords and usernames.

To reduce the chances of usernames and passwords being compromised:

- they should be as long as possible and have a minimum character length;
- they should be alphanumeric, including a combination of letters, numbers and symbols;
- password/username files should be encrypted and stored securely;
- staff shouldn't use the same password/username for multiple software applications;

- default passwords need to be changed;
- passwords need to be changed on a regular basis.

c) SQL (Structured Query Language) injections – SQL code is written into a form on a website to retrieve information from the database illicitly.
d) Denial of service (DOS) attacks – this is when an attacker makes a network of computers send lots of data requests to a server, causing it to crash so that no one can request information from the database.
e) URL (Web address) parameter attacks – parameters in a website's URL can be used to retrieve information from the database. This can be done via SQL or manipulating the URL.

Network threats

a) Sniffing – this is the monitoring of data packets on networks.
b) Spoofing – this involves manipulating data to impersonate a legitimate user in order to gain access to a network or deceive other individuals to obtain information to be used in illegal activities.
c) 'Man in the middle' attacks – data being sent between users can be intercepted, compromised and manipulated.

As more and more data is being accessed by mobile devices and increasingly being held on the cloud, network security is becoming an ever-increasing concern.

Social engineering   Hackers can engineer electronic or non-electronic methods to gain information from legitimate users in order to gain access to a computer network or other organisational resources.

DISPOSAL AND SECURITY OF DATA WITHIN THE ORGANISATION

How an organisation disposes of information is just as important, whether it is electronic or hard copy.

Hard copy information   Hard copy information should be stored, distributed and disposed of securely. Most organisations have a confidential waste policy which stipulates what must be disposed of by a third party specialising in the destruction of sensitive data.

Electronic information   If laptops or PCs are to be recycled or destroyed, the organisation needs to implement policies to make sure all data has been wiped clean from the devices.

Just because someone deletes a file does not mean it has been completely erased from the hard drive.

There are a wide variety of file shredders and computer cleaning utilities an organisation can use to make sure no data can be retrieved from the computers it disposes of.

2. Risk analysis

After the threats, risks, vulnerabilities, impacts and probabilities of each threat have been identified, we can assess the likelihood of the risks occurring.

When undertaking this stage, quantitative or qualitative methods or a mixture of both can be used to assess each risk.

Calculating risk

This stage of the process is concerned with calculating risk or trying to determine the effect it will have on the organisation so that a decision can be made on the course of action required to mitigate it.

Risk, as established earlier, is the combination of the impact and probability of a breach occurring.

A numeric value or risk score can be assigned to each individual risk:

Risk = Impact × Probability of the risk occurring

A value between 1 and 10 is determined for both Impact and Probability, 1 being low and 10 high. The values are then multiplied to produce a risk score.

For example, an organisation may be assessing the risk of a rogue employee stealing data. It has assessed this threat and determined that the probability of this threat occurring has a value of 2 and the impact on the organisation has a value of 8:

Risk of a rogue employee stealing data = Impact × Probability of the risk occurring
Risk of a rogue employee stealing data = 8 × 2
Risk score = 16

The higher the value, the higher the risk to the organisation.

3. Risk prioritisation

When the analysis of different risks has been completed, the organisation should be in a position to prioritise what risks need to be addressed and in what order to do so.

Using our example of a rogue employee stealing data having a probability value of 2 and an impact value of 8, the threat can be mapped on an probability impact matrix (as shown in Figure 9). This can then be used to show what risks should be prioritised depending on the level of threat to the organisation's data.

The threats with the highest probability and highest impact should be dealt with first.

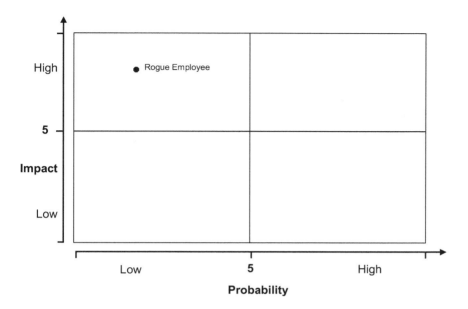

Figure 9 Probability impact matrix

Source: The Open University, Introduction to Cyber Security (Online Course) – https://www.future-learn.com/courses/introduction-to-cyber-security/9/steps/122046.

Risk control

4. Risk management planning

This stage is concerned with developing and implementing how the organisation intends to deal with risks and threats.

5. Risk mitigation/resolution

This stage is concerned with what action is undertaken by an organisation to mitigate or reduce particular risks.

Broadly speaking, there are four strategies an organisation can adopt to do this, as outlined by the PCI Security Standards Council (November 2012, p.15).[48]

Risk reduction

Risk reduction could include updating software, reviewing internet access policies and procedures, and having a password policy.

---

48 PCI Security Standards Council (November 2012), *Information Supplement: PCI DSS Risk Assessment Guidelines Version 1.0*, Wakefield, UK: PCI Security Standards Council.

Any risk that is left after a measure has been implemented to mitigate it is called the residual risk.

Risk avoidance

Risk avoidance involves avoiding engaging in activities that will put the business at risk of being exposed to additional threats.

Measures could include avoiding the use of suppliers who do not have adequate security procedures in place to handle the business's data.

Risk acceptance

Risk acceptance involves the organisation accepting the risks associated with its business practices as falling within acceptable limits, including any costs and consequences if a worst case scenario occurs.

According to The Open Group (2010, p.26),[49] the following considerations should apply when developing risk acceptance criteria:

- business criteria;
- legal and regulatory aspects;
- operational considerations;
- technological aspects;
- financial considerations;
- social and humanitarian factors.

When developing levels for risk acceptance, The Open Group (2010, pp.25–26)[50] recommends that the following points should be considered:

- Risk acceptance levels may apply to different aspects of risk.
- Risk acceptance criteria may take into consideration how long the risk will be expected to exist.
- Risk acceptance may have multiple thresholds for each risk and threat to an organisation. For example, there may be a normal level of operating risk. In some business operating circumstances, the risk level may rise. However, due to business circumstances, this new risk level will still be acceptable.
- Risk acceptance criteria can be developed by analysing the potential benefits of that risk for the organisation – for example, the trade-off of profit against the risk.
- Risk acceptance criteria may include future action that is to be taken by the organisation. This could include things like implementing new risk prevention or reduction technology or developing/re-engineering new business processes.

49 The Open Group (2010), *Technical Guide FAIR – ISO/IEC27005 Cookbook*, Reading, UK: The Open Group.
50 The Open Group (2010), *Technical Guide FAIR – ISO/IEC27005 Cookbook*, Reading, UK: The Open Group.

Risk sharing with third parties

This usually arises when the organisation is engaged with third-party suppliers and vendors.

The PCI Security Standards Council (November 2012, p.16)[51] specifies three areas to consider when dealing with third-party organisations:

a) Introduction of risk – using third parties will bring additional risk to the organisation. This could include the development of new software and processes being implemented.
b) Managed risk – this is concerned with outsourcing of work to a third party.
c) Shared risk – the sharing of a business process with another organisation.

6. Monitor and review

When the risks have been assessed, the necessary course of action has been chosen by an organisation and the appropriate measures have been implemented by the organisation to deal with the risk, the proposed solutions to resolve those threats need to be evaluated.

The risk assessment process must be ongoing continuous process to ensure that the organisation can mitigate threats and ensure that the solutions it has implemented have successfully resolved them.

The PDCA model can be used to implement a risk management methodology and process. PDCA stands for:

- Plan
- Do
- Check
- Act.

PDCA was developed by Edwards Deming as methodology to continually improve performance. It can be applied to dealing with risks within an organisation in the following way:

Plan – assess the threats, impacts and vulnerabilities the organisation faces. These will include all internal and external threats, and will look at technology, processes and the staff within the organisation.

Do – this stage involves the implementation of controls, procedures and policies to reduce the risks.

Check – the risk assessment metrics implemented should be assessed on a continuous basis.

Act – if a particular control to mitigate a risk is not working, then:

---

51 PCI Security Standards Council (November 2012), *Information Supplement: PCI DSS Risk Assessment Guidelines Version 1.0*, Wakefield, UK: PCI Security Standards Council.

- try another solution/control;
- re-engineer the chosen solution;
- apply additional preventative measures to reduce the threat.

When the risk assessment has been completed, the organisation should be able to:

- identify all the risks/threats it faces;
- calculate the level of each risk/threat;
- prioritise and plan how to deal with the risks;
- implement the necessary strategies to mitigate those risks.

This methodology is also covered by The Open Group (2010, p.4).[52]

Data breach/security contingency planning

The organisation should plan for the worst case scenario that a data breach does happen.

Why do data breaches occur?

Guidance on Data Security Breach Management Version 2.1 (Information Commissioner's Office (UK), 2012, p.2)[53] explains possible reasons why data breaches occur:

- loss or theft of data or equipment on which data is stored;
- inappropriate access controls allowing unauthorised use;
- equipment failure;
- human error;
- unforeseen circumstances, such as a fire or flood;
- hacking attacks;
- 'blagging' offences, where information is obtained by deceiving the organisation who holds it.

The reasons outlined above come down to failures or breakdowns in technology, processes or people.

The effects of a not dealing with a data breach

The effects of not dealing with a data breach correctly can include:

- damage to a brand's image and loss of long-term trust among customers who have trusted the organisation with their information;

---

52 The Open Group (2010), *Technical Guide FAIR – ISO/IEC27005 Cookbook*, Reading, UK: The Open Group.
53 Information Commissioner's Office (UK) (2012), *Guidance on Data Security Breach Management Version 2.1*, http://webarchive.nationalarchives.gov.uk/20130604230652/http://www.ico.org. uk/youth/sitecore/content/Home/for_organisations/data_protection/~/media/documents/library/ Data_Protection/Practical_application/guidance_on_data_security_breach_management.ashx.

- legal consequences;
- financial costs may include loss of sales, drop in share price or fines from regulatory/government agencies for not implementing the relevant steps to prevent the data breach.

Dealing with a security/data breach

A data breach plan needs to be developed and implemented within the organisation as part of its overall contingency planning processes.

Guidance on Data Security Breach Management Version 2.1 (Information Commissioner's Office (UK), 2012, p.2)[54] sets out a process which includes:

- containment and recovery;
- assessment of ongoing risk;
- notification of breach;
- evaluation and response.

Other security-related topics

Data breach insurance policies

It is now possible for organisations to take out insurance policies against the possibility of costs resulting from data breaches.

Data seeding

The data needs to be seeded with deliberately false records to alert the organisation that data may have been appropriated by members of staff who have moved on to jobs elsewhere but are continuing to use the organisation's data.

For example, the organisation can be alerted to a breach by seeding false contact information, which will have a legitimate email or postal address or telephone number that can be monitored.

Ownership of the data needs to be communicated to all employees of the organisation, or even in some cases written into employment contracts.

Testing security measure implementation within an organisation

There are plenty of IT security organisations that can be engaged to test the organisation's security policies and look for possible loopholes in its security measures.

54 Information Commissioner's Office (UK) (2012), *Guidance on Data Security Breach Management Version 2.1*, http://webarchive.nationalarchives.gov.uk/20130604230652/http://www.ico.org.uk/youth/sitecore/content/Home/for_organisations/data_protection/~/media/documents/library/Data_Protection/Practical_application/guidance_on_data_security_breach_management.ashx.

Obtaining an industry standard accreditation in security

The organisation could obtain an industry standard accreditation in security to show customers and clients that it has put in place the necessary precautions to make sure their data is secure.

ISO 27001 is an example of a recognised industry security accreditation.

Case study

Data XYZ PLC has undertaken a review of its security procedures regarding the use of data, and the following security situation has been identified.

IT software is regularly updated with the latest patches, the corporate firewall is also updated, no information is stored in the cloud, and threats to the organisation are regularly reviewed by IT security.

Employees are accessing the CRM platform via their laptops or mobile phones across an insecure network.

Storage devices such as USB sticks are being lost and are not encrypted.

When sending data to third-party fulfilment organisations, the data is not always encrypted.

Employees are able to download information from the CRM database and store it on their desktops and local computer drives.

It has come to the attention of the organisation that customers may have been receiving mailings from ex-members of staff who have joined a rival organisation and may have appropriated information from the CRM database and taken it with them after leaving Data XYZ PLC.

Confidential information is disposed of with the regular waste, and no procedures exist to clean electronic devices before they are disposed of or recycled.

Possible improvements in this case study scenario

Data XYZ PLC seems to be failing not only in some of the technical aspects, but also in implementing any business processes regarding data security.

Implementing the following measures and procedures could improve the security of its data.

Data should be encrypted when sending it to third-party organisations or accessing it from outside the organisation. This could be done using a third-party encryption program, or if a third-party provider has its own secure network, this could be used as well.

If employees need access to the CRM database, this should be via work-only devices connected to a secure network.

Procedures, processes and guidelines covering the encryption of data on work and storage devices like laptops and USB sticks need to be implemented and communicated to all staff as and when necessary via email or the company intranet, and should be part of a new employee's induction process.

Access rights to information on the CRM database needs to be reviewed so that only those who need to download data are able to do so. All other staff can be restricted to viewing the information they need onscreen.

Data needs to be seeded in the CRM database so that the company will be alerted about possible theft of information when staff leave the organisation and the appropriate action can then be taken.

Employees need to be made aware that the data is an asset of the organisation, and the consequences for appropriating this asset without its consent need to be made clear, possibly as part of their employment contracts.

Data XYZ PLC needs to arrange for the safe disposal of confidential hard copy information, such as by hiring a specialist firm to destroy the relevant information.

Procedures to clean electronic devices before they are disposed of need to be introduced.

Data XYZ PLC should also try to attain a recognised security standard and work with third-party organisations to improve security.

As part of this process, a security audit should be undertaken which will highlight any security flaws and possible improvements to existing procedures.

A data breach team and response plan need to be developed and implemented within the organisation to prepare for any data breaches. The plan needs to be communicated to relevant members of staff who will be involved in co-ordinating and managing the organisation's response. The procedure needs to be reviewed and updated on a regular basis, and should be part of the organisation's overall business contingency planning process.

Data security should be built into the organisation's overall data governance strategy.

As an additional precaution, Data XYZ PLC could take out an insurance policy against any possible data breaches.

Security management processes, plans and risk assessment for the organisation's data need to be monitored and reviewed.

The necessary strategies and controls to avoid or reduce the risk of a security or data breach of the CRM database need to be followed on a continuous basis.

Summary

Security considerations need to be an integral part from the conception of the design of the CRM platform through to how the data is accessed and finally disposed of.

All security threats, both internal and external, need to be assessed so that the necessary measures can be implemented by the organisation to make its data as secure as possible.

A risk assessment must be carried out on the dangers of a security/data breach of the CRM database occurring. There are many risk assessment methodologies and frameworks that can be used to do this.

A risk or threat to an organisation is a combination of elements that include asset, impact, probability of that risk occurring and vulnerability.

Risk can be defined as the probability of the risk occurring combined with the impact the risk will have on the organisation.

The risk management process includes:

- identifying the risks and threats to the organisation's data;
- analysing those risks and threats;
- prioritising the threats and risks to mitigate;
- implementing solutions to address the threats and risks;
- reviewing and monitoring the success of the solutions;
- continuously assessing the threats and risks.

A model for risk prevention and assessment that could also be used is the Demming PDCA model, which includes the stages of:

- Plan
- Do
- Check
- Act.

The risk assessment process needs to be undertaken on a continuous basis to take into consideration the changing business environment the organisation operates in and the changing threats and challenges it will face.

A data breach plan needs to be developed and implemented within the organisation.

Guidance on Data Security Breach Management Version 2.1 (Information Commissioner's Office (UK), 2012, p.2)[55] sets out a process which includes:

- containment and recovery;
- assessment of ongoing risks;
- notification of breach;
- evaluation and response.

A data breach team needs to be set up to co-ordinate and manage responses to data breaches.

The responsibilities of the data breach team will include:

- planning how the organisation will respond to data breaches;
- drawing up IT response, communication and investigation plans;

---

55 Information Commissioner's Office (UK) (2012), *Guidance on Data Security Breach Management Version 2.1*, http://webarchive.nationalarchives.gov.uk/20130604230652/http://www.ico.org. uk/youth/sitecore/content/Home/for_organisations/data_protection/~/media/documents/library/ Data_Protection/Practical_application/guidance_on_data_security_breach_management.ashx.

- ensuring the necessary staff and technical resources are made available or that additional resources can be brought in to help deal with any breach;
- liaising and co-ordinating with third-party providers, government agencies and law enforcement to deal with data breaches effectively;
- ensuring that these plans are already in place before any breach occurs and conducting regular reviews and updates.

DATA STORAGE

This section will cover:

- the different ways of storing CRM data;
- the factors to be considered when deciding upon a storage system for the CRM data.

The two main concerns with data storage are where the data is stored and how this is done.

Where the data is stored

There are two main options for where the organisation's data could be stored:

a) In-house – data can be stored in the organisation's own data centres and data-base servers.
b) Third-party data centres – data can be stored by a third-party organisation.

Cloud technology

Cloud technology can also be used for data storage. The types of cloud technology available are public, private and hybrid.

How the data is stored

Data can be stored in broadly two types of database: RDBMS and NoSQL:

- RDBMS (Rational Database Management System) – in this method, data is stored in tables that can be indexed and linked to each other.
- NoSQL (Not only SQL) – there are a variety of NoSQL database platforms, including:
  - document;
  - graph;

- o   key value store;
- o   column store.

Some database platforms seek to combine the benefits of NoSQL and RDBMS technology into one system.

Factors to consider for data storage

Factors that need to be considered when considering data storage include:

a)   Cost – what are the cost implications of the organisation maintaining and storing its data itself compared to using a third party to do so.
b)   Security – any security aspects and concerns about the storage of data need to be addressed.
c)   Technical expertise – does the organisation have the necessary technical expertise and resources available to maintain and service the data stored? If not, using a third party's data storage facilities could be an option.
d)   Variety/types of data to be stored – is the type of data mainly text-based? Are other media and file types going to be stored?
e)   Velocity – how quickly will it be necessary to enter and extract data to and from the database? This may form part of the technical/performance requirements of the database when selecting a suitable solution for your organisation.
f)   Capacity/volume of data – does the organisation have the capacity to store and maintain all its data in its current data storage platform? Will it be able to cope with expected future demands for storage?
g)   Performance/technical requirements – these include technical factors like how quickly the data needs to written/read (saved/extracted).

Data retention and record management plan

An electronic data retention plan will need to be developed and implemented. It should be closely linked to the organisation's record management guidelines and procedures because anything archived, deleted and retained in electronic format needs to be consistent with what the organisation archives, deletes and retains in hard copy format.

The organisation should have guidelines and procedures for record management in place for managing hard copy information, including:

a)   Schedules – a timetable for archiving and deleting of information needs to be implemented.
b)   Where the information is to be stored – the organisation could use its own facilities or a third-party storage provider.
c)   Transportation of information – the hard copy information should be transported in a secure environment to a secure site for storage or disposal.

d) Processing hard copy information – the storage of hard copy information while it's being processed needs to be considered. No confidential or sensitive information should be left on desks or in an insecure environment.
e) Responsibility for archiving and deleting information – who within the organisation is responsible for ensuring that information in electronic and hard copy formats is archived and deleted properly?
f) Electronic filing of hard copies – hard copies may be scanned before being moved off-site and archived. How this information is to be managed needs to be determined.
g) Recording of archived and deleted files – a system needs to be introduced so that the organisation has a record of what files have been archived and deleted, where they can be located and who has them, for auditing and possibly legal reasons.

Factors similar to the storage of electronic information like cost, security and capacity will determine what solutions for the storage of hard copy information will be implemented within the organisation.

Other factors such as the organisation's legal obligations regarding data will also need to be taken into consideration.

The record management plan needs to be consistent with the information held in the CRM database.

Contingency planning

Any contingency plan will involve deciding where copies or backups of electronic data are stored in case a man-made or natural disaster occurs that affects the organisation's daily business activities.

This is to ensure that any disruption experienced by the organisation does not lead to a loss of data and a long delay in accessing and retrieving the information it needs to meet its objectives.

Case study

Data XYZ PLC is receiving and dealing with a variety of types of data concerning its customers, and is concerned whether the CRM platform based on RDBMS technology is appropriate to deal with this.

The processes for management, storage and disposal of information have also been highlighted as vulnerable to security breaches.

Possible improvements in this case study scenario

Data XYZ PLC could undertake a study comparing the advantages and disadvantages of NoSQL technology compared to RDBMS databases to see whether the current system best serves its requirements.

Procedures when data is deleted, archived and retrieved need to be revised to ensure compliance with data legislation and reduce the likelihood of security breaches.

Summary

A number of data storage options are available to organisations.

Data can be stored in RDBMS or NoSQL database platforms.

It can be stored in-house or by a third-party provider.

The organisation needs to develop a data retention plan that covers how it retains, stores, deletes and archives both electronic and hard copy information.

It will need to draw up a specification, both from a technical and business perspective, to adequately assess the options that are suitable for its data storage requirements.

DATA SUPPLIERS

> This section will cover:
>
> • issues when dealing with third-party data suppliers.

When implementing or administering the CRM database, the organisation may need to use external suppliers or third parties, perhaps in the initial building of the CRM platform or by using third-party software and services, such as data hosting, technical support, data cleaning services, the purchase of email software and even the use of temporary staff to ensure the work of the data team can be undertaken.

It is important that guidelines and procedures are developed and a process is implemented so that the organisation can identify, obtain and implement the third-party services and products it requires for the CRM database platform to function.

Selecting a supplier of a product or CRM platform usually involves some kind of tendering process where the organisation will ask several suppliers to bid for a contract.

Factors to consider when selecting third-party suppliers

a) Transparency of the process – whatever process is used by the organisation to select an external supplier, it needs to be transparent so it's clear how a decision was reached.

b) Criteria and scope of work – the desired features and scope of work of the product or service need to be defined, to be used as a criteria for making a choice.

c) Financial costs of the product or service – all costs associated with the product or service need to be identified. These include the initial cost of the product/ service and the running costs.

d) Contracts/service level agreements – when a product or service is selected, the contract/service level agreement must outline each party's responsibilities, such as the schedule and scope of the work to be undertaken.

e) Time constraints – this could include the length of contract both parties will enter into if a certain product or service is selected.

f) Auditing of the process – this needs to be carried out so that the organisation can ensure it has obtained the service/product it required, possible problems are not repeated in the future, and that it is getting value for money.

Having a process and guidelines in place for selecting external suppliers will enable the organisation to select the services or products it needs while remaining accountable to stakeholders in explaining how decisions were made and why particular products or services were chosen.

The following points also need to be considered to ensure an effective working relationship with third-party suppliers:

- Keep a record of any issues or problems when using a supplier or service.
- Make sure you have a point of contact within the third-party provider to discuss problems and issues the organisation is experiencing.
- Hold regular meetings with the supplier to discuss issues and problem areas.
- Implement procedures with the third-party provider to resolve any data anomalies and issues that may occur, to ensure that the same mistakes, problems and issues are not constantly being repeated.

DAMA (2009, p.161)[56] outlines a possible methodology when dealing with third-party suppliers: the RACI (Responsible, Accountable, Consulted, and Informed) matrix. This can be used as a basis for any contracts or agreements between the organisation and data suppliers which need to be reviewed at regular intervals.

Case study

Data XYZ PLC has had a supplier who provides data services on its behalf for a considerable number of years. The supplier has never had to tender for the work it undertakes for Data XYZ PLC.

---

56 *DAMA-Data Management Body of Knowledge* ©.

There have also been issues with the supplier, such as missing SLAs for the delivery of the data and errors causing delays to data being updated on the CRM database.

Possible improvements in this case study scenario

The contract to provide data services for Data XYZ PLC should be reviewed on a regular basis.

When the contract is to be reviewed or work put out to tender, a specification should be drawn up outlining the criteria for any supplier.

When working with the existing supplier, regular meetings and reviews should be held.

Any problems with the supplier should be documented and relevant solutions sought during these regular reviews.

If data provided by a third-party supplier for importation into the CRM platform is below the standard required, procedures and workflows need to be agreed to update and improve the supplier's systems so that the same errors do not continually occur.

Summary

When considering employing third-party providers on any project, the organisation must implement a process to ensure that the criteria for selection are clearly defined and completely transparent to ensure that the best provider is selected.

Issues organisations need to be aware of when selecting a third-party provider include:

- legal and contractual issues;
- financial considerations;
- the scope of work to be undertaken.

DATA LEGISLATION

This section will cover:

- the importance of being aware that data legislation can affect all areas of data management and varies depending on where in the world the organisation operates.

Important issues that need to be addressed by any organisation are the legal and compliance issues surrounding its use of data.

When it comes to data legislation, where the organisation is based and operates in the world affects its legal responsibilities and the regulations it needs to comply with when managing data. For example, the United Kingdom has the Data Protection Act, which all organisations must abide by when using data, but not every country in the world has a similar Act.

Data legislation can cover the whole data lifecycle, from data capture (collection), storage/processing/maintenance of data to analysis/interpretation/reporting and data reprocessing, and affects all aspects of data management.

The detail of global data legislation would be a subject for a book all by itself, and falls outside the scope of this volume.

If in doubt, consult your organisation's legal department or a government or industry body for help and advice on data legislation.

Failure to comply with data legislation can lead to financial penalties and damage an organisation's brand.

Case study

Data XYZ PLC has no understanding of and has not even considered the implications of its legal obligations when holding personal data about customers and clients.

Possible improvements in this case study scenario

The company needs to investigate what legislation it needs to comply with in regard to data, ascertain whether its in breach of that legislation, and make any changes to working practices accordingly to meet its legal obligations.

A culture of data governance needs to be implemented from the top down to ensure that employees are aware of their responsibilities while managing personal data and the negative impact a data breach would have on the organisation. Data governance and responsibilities when managing personal data should be discussed when a member of staff is inducted into the organisation.

More specific training courses can be undertaken by staff regarding aspects of data legislation if required for their roles.

This should ultimately lead to the organisation having a dedicated member of staff/working group to act as a point of contact regarding all matters to do with data legislation and governance.

Procedures and guidelines should be formulated to address any legal obligations the organisation has in regard to data.

Summary

Legal requirements impact on all aspects of data management and the data lifecycle, from data capture (collection), storage/processing/maintenance of data to analysis/interpretation/reporting and data reprocessing.

The legal requirements of an organisation will depend on where in the world it is located and operates.

Failure to comply with data legislation may not only impact the organisation financially, but also damage its brand.

A culture of data governance needs to be fostered within the organisation at all levels of its structure and at each stage of the data lifecycle.

SUMMARY

> This section recaps the main points that have been covered in this guide.

Database platforms

There are broadly three options for organisations when choosing a CRM platform:

- bespoke in-house-built platforms;
- off-the-shelf platforms;
- open source platforms.

Data management needs to be implemented through all stages of the data lifecycle, which comprises data capture (collection), storage/processing/maintenance of data, analysis/interpretation/reporting and data reprocessing.

Implementation and development of the CRM database

Implementing a CRM database in an organisation requires a clear methodology to be adopted with clearly defined steps. When the CRM platform has finally been deployed within the organisation, it is not the end of the process.

Managing, maintaining, developing and ensuring the database meets the needs of the organisation in a changing business environment is an ongoing process.

With the appropriate staff and resources to meet these challenges, the CRM database can provide benefits to the organisation such as:

- improved knowledge about customers and the business environment the organisation operates in;
- improved workflows within the organisation;
- improved decision-making at executive and operational levels;
- better targeting of key groups to help achieve business objectives;
- financial gains through reduced costs and higher financial returns.

The CRM database and data should be an asset and an aid to staff in carrying out their daily responsibilities and tasks within the workplace and supporting the organisation in achieving its overall goals and objectives.

Staff and the organisation should not feel that the data and CRM platform are barriers to overcome in order to succeed in the business environment they are competing in.

Data capture (collection) and data quality

A data capture (collection) process and strategy will need to be developed within the organisation to cover aspects from how data is collected through to how the data is to be stored – for example, on the CRM platform.

Data quality is a multi-dimensional concept that needs to be addressed by the organisation as a whole through a constant, ongoing process.

A data quality framework needs to be adopted so that the data within the CRM platform continuously meets the requirements and data quality standards defined by the organisation to enable it to achieve its goals.

Data team management

The data team needs to have a formalised organisational structure so that it can undertake the tasks and responsibilities associated with managing and administering the CRM platform successfully and efficiently. How the team fits into the rest of its department and the organisation as a whole needs to be addressed.

Workflows into and out of the data team need to be assessed to ensure that they are working efficiently to meet the organisation's data needs.

Data tasks the organisation will not be undertaking itself can be contracted out to third-party providers.

Data plans

A data plan needs to be developed for the CRM platform so that the organisation is able to meet it overall objectives.

What is contained within the data plan will be linked to the goals of the organisation, and will change accordingly when the objectives of the organisation change.

Data audits

A data audit framework needs to developed by the CRM data team.

Data audits need to be carried out regularly to ensure the data on the CRM platform meets the requirements of the organisation so that its objectives can be achieved.

Data audits:

- help to improve the quality of data held by an organisation;
- assist in finding any data gaps within the organisation's data sets;
- help identify possible improvements that can be made to workflows and processes in regard to the management of the CRM platform.

Data migrations

A structured approach needs to be adopted when transferring data from one system to another, and requires scheduling and planning of the resources and personnel necessary for the project to succeed.

How the project will affect the rest of the organisation needs to be effectively managed and communicated throughout the organisation.

Data security

When it comes to data security, the following issues need to be addressed:

- Who has access to the data, and what data do they have access to?
- Internal and external threats need to be considered.
- Security is not only a technical issue. Employees need to be made aware of procedures and guidelines regarding data security, and these need to be enforced.
- Data/security breach contingency plans need to be developed so that if the worst case scenario occurs, the organisation knows how to react.
- Security of the data should be a consideration when choosing or developing any CRM database solution.
- Possible security threats need to be assessed at each stage of the data lifecycle. This may include setting up a data breach team consisting of members of different departments, including IT, marketing and senior management.

Data storage

Types of data storage platforms need to be assessed by the organisation to ensure that they can meet its current and future needs.

Where the data is stored, either in-house or using a third-party organisation, needs to be considered.

A process for the retention, deletion, archiving, storage and disposal of electronic and hard copy information needs to be developed.

Data suppliers

A process needs to be implemented for selecting third-party providers to undertake work on behalf of the organisation.

Contracts should be drawn up between the organisation and supplier, which will include the scope of the work, schedules, legal considerations, SLAs and financial aspects of the work to be carried out, such as cost of the service/work to be undertaken, and any additional penalties or costs either party may be liable for.

The process needs to be transparent and auditable so that the organisation can justify its decision to select a particular third party to undertake the work required.

Data legislation

Organisations should be aware of what legislation applies to their management and use of data.

Mailings and reporting

A mailing and reporting process, guidelines, procedures and schedules need to be established and implemented.

Who will be undertaking the reporting and mailing tasks and how they are to be carried out need to be defined.

Documentation

Documentation needs to be developed covering the guidelines/procedures/workflows in the following areas:

- reporting and analysis;
- mailings;
- data audits;
- data quality;
- CRM database administration tasks;
- data plans;
- legal and data compliance;
- development of the CRM platform;
- security procedures.

These need to be reviewed and updated regularly to enable the organisation to:

- exploit the data set to its full potential;
- improve working practices and workflows within the organisation;
- reduce organisational costs.

CONCLUSION

It should be remembered that there are two aspects to the term 'database management'.

The database is the tool that will be used by the organisation to manage its data and help achieve its goals and objectives.

The CRM database is a tool to help manage the data set or data asset, therefore the CRM database is only as good as the data it contains.

Management deals with how you use this technological tool.

The reason I highlight this point is that you can have the best CRM database technology in the world, but if it is poorly managed, it will be completely useless in assisting the organisation to meet its objectives and goals.

It should also be highlighted that data management, just like CRM database development, needs to be a constant, ongoing process of review, development and improvement if the organisation is to achieve its goals.

Even though this book has concentrated on aspects and issues relating to CRM platforms, the principles it has covered can be applied to the entire organisation:

- data quality framework;
- awareness of data legislation issues;
- data audit frameworks;
- data risk assessments;
- dealing with data breaches;
- dealing with third-party suppliers.

Bibliography

Books

Baxter, K. (2010) *Risk Management*, London: Pearson Education Limited.

Beamish, K. (2001) *Marketing Operations*, Oxford: Butterworth-Heinemann.

DAMA (2009) *DAMA-Data Management Body of Knowledge ©*, Denville, NJ: Technics Publications.

English, L.P. (2009) *Information Quality Applied: Best Practices for Improving Business Information, Processes, and Systems*, Chichester, UK: Wiley.

Loshin, D. (2011) *The Practitioner's Guide to Data Quality Improvement*, Burlington, MA: Morgan Kaufmann.

Phipps, R. & Simmons, C. (2002) *The Marketing Customer Interface*, Oxford: Butterworth-Heinemann.

Worsam, M. (2002) *Effective Management for Marketing*, Oxford: Butterworth-Heinemann.

Online resources

Epicor (2005) *Strategies for a Successful CRM Implementation: A Guide for Small and Medium Sized Enterprises*, Bracknell, UK: Epicor Software Corporation. Available at http://hosteddocs.toolbox.com/strategies%20for%20a%20successful%20crm%20 implementation.pdf. Accessed 21 August 2018.

Information Commissioner's Office (UK) (2012) *Guidance on Data Security Breach Management Version 2.1*. Available at http://webarchive.nationalarchives.gov.uk/ 20130604230652/http://www.ico.org.uk/youth/sitecore/content/Home/for_organisations/ data_protection/~/media/documents/library/Data_Protection/Practical_application/ guidance_on_data_security_breach_management.ashx. Accessed 17 October 2018.

Jones, S., Ross, S. & Ruusalepp, R. (May 2009) *Data Audit Framework Methodology, Version 1.8*, Glasgow, UK: HATII. Available at www.data-audit.eu/DAF_Methodology. pdf. Accessed 21 August 2018.

Leek, J. (2013) 'Six Types of Analysis Every Data Scientist Should Know'. Available at http://datascientistinsights.com/2013/01/29/six-types-of-analyses-every-data-scientist-should-know/. Accessed 21 August 2018.

Leland, E. & Salter, J., FivePaths, LLC (n.d.) *The Six Elements of Successful CRM Selection and Implementation: How to Stay Focused and Cover Your Bases When Choosing and Setting Up a Customer Relationship Management System*. Available at https://www. fivepaths.com/sites/default/files/resources/six_elements_of_successful_crm_selection_ and_implementation-fivepaths.pdf. Accessed 21 August 2018.

PCI Security Standards Council (November 2012) *Information Supplement: PCI DSS Risk Assessment Guidelines Version 1.0*, Wakefield, UK: PCI Security Standards Council. Available at www.pcisecuritystandards.org/documents/PCI_DSS_Risk_Assmt_Guidelines_v1.pdf. Accessed 21 August 2018.

Schneier, B. (2013) 'People, Process and Technology'. Available at www.schneier.com/blog/archives/2013/01/people_process.html. Accessed 21 August 2018.

The Open Group (2010) *Technical Guide FAIR – ISO/IEC 27005 Cookbook*, Reading, UK: The Open Group. Available at https://publications.opengroup.org/c103 (login required). Accessed 21 August 2018.

The Open University (n.d.) *Introduction to Cyber Security* (online course). Available at http://www.open.edu/openlearn/futurelearn/cyber-security. Accessed 21 August 2018.

Other material

DataFlux Corporation (2003) *Data Profiling: The Foundation for Data Management*, Cary, NC: DataFlux Corporation.

Premier Inc. (2013) *Examples of Types of Process Maps*, Charlotte, NC: Premier Inc.

Appendices

Appendix 1: Data mailing form

Contact information

Date:
Name of requester:
Position:
Department:
Email address:
Phone extension number:

Mailing information

Date data required by:
Mailing ID (unique prefix):
Name of Mailing:
Mailing number:
File format data required in:
Exclusions:
Mailing type (post/email/text):

Mailing segments

Segment ID	Mailing segment name	Mailing segment description	Query name	Data file URL

Data information

Completed by:
Date completed:
Data checked by:
Date checked:
Date data sent:

Appendix 2: Electronic data mailing form

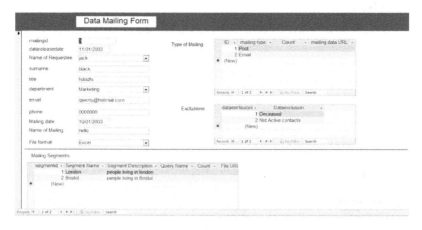

Appendix 3: Database structure of data mailing form

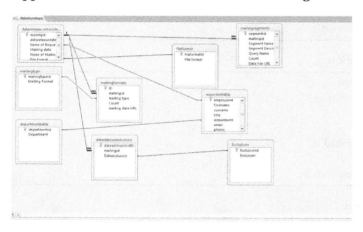

Index

For Product Safety Concerns and Information please contact our EU
representative GPSR@taylorandfrancis.com
Taylor & Francis Verlag GmbH, Kaufingerstraße 24, 80331 München, Germany